名作映画でTOEIC® (4)
めざせ！470

The Wizard of Oz

Boost your skills for the TOEIC® Test with *The Wizard of Oz*

Kay Nakago

Shigeru Ozawa

Akiko Ohta

Isabelle Bilodeau

Beverley Curran

EIHŌSHA

─── オーディオ CD について ───

本テキストには、学生用オーディオ CD が付属する。なお、学生用 CD とは別に、練習問題の朗読や解答を含む教員用 CD も用意してある。

Ⓢ　　学生用 CD（本テキスト付属）

Ⓣ1 **Ⓣ2**　　教員用 CD（教員用 CD は T1 と T2 の 2 枚組）

は じ め に

　「名作映画で TOEIC®」シリーズは、『カサブランカ』、『シャレード』、『第三の男』に続き、本書で四冊目である。映画のストーリーを楽しみながら、英語のリーディング力とリスニング力の向上をめざすというこのシリーズは、幸い、採用していただいた全国の先生方からも、授業を受講している学生のみなさんからも好評を博してきた。第四作は、映画『オズの魔法使』（*The Wizard of Oz* 1939 年）に基づき、TOEIC 470 点をめざす平均的な大学生に向けて制作された。なお、本書は 2016 年 5 月に導入された TOEIC 新形式に対応している。

　映画『オズの魔法使』は、1939 年のアカデミー賞で作曲賞、歌曲賞、特別賞を受賞した名作である。アメリカ合衆国の国家的機関アメリカン・フィルム・インスティチュート（American Film Institute: AFI）による「歴代名画ベスト 100」では第 6 位、「歴代名ミュージカル映画」では第 3 位に選ばれている。主演のジュディ・ガーランド（Judy Garland）が演じるドロシー（Dorothy）が歌う「虹の彼方に」（*Over the Rainbow*）は「歴代名歌曲ベスト 100」（AFI）第 1 位、「20 世紀の名曲」（全米レコード協会）第 1 位を獲得している。また、ドロシーの台詞 "We're not in Kansas anymore."（もうカンザスにいるわけではない）や "There's no place like home."（我が家にまさるところはない）などは名台詞としても知られ、一般の英和辞書にも収録されている。（ただし、"There's no place like home." はもとは、アメリカ人劇作家ジョン・ハワード・ペイン（John Howard Payne, 1791-1852）が作詞した「埴生の宿」（*Home, Sweet Home*）の歌詞の一部である。）アメリカ映画の中の台詞には『オズの魔法使』からの引用も多い。このような観点から、この映画は、まさしく、アメリカ文化の一部を形成していると言っても過言ではない。映画を題材として英語を学習するということは、アメリカ文化や英語文化を学ぶということでもある。

　なお、映画の日本語タイトルは送り仮名が入る「魔法使い」ではなく「魔法使」が正式であるため、本書では『オズの魔法使』と表記する。また、*Over the Rainbow* は「虹の彼方へ」とされることもあるが、本書では、「虹の彼方に」と表記する。

　本書は、映画を題材として、英語力をさまざまな角度から身に付けるというシリーズの目的を堅持して執筆された。Act 1 から 12 までのそれぞれの Act には、英語リスニングのコツ（tips）を音声学の観点から段階的に学ぶ Listening Tips と、文法の基本事項を網羅的に確認する Grammar Training がある。リスニングセクションについては、別途、Dictation コーナーが設けられている。どこを正しく聞き取れたか、

どこがどのように聞き取れなかったかを把握し、リスニング能力の向上に努めていただきたい。Part 6 や Part 7 については、随所に、この映画の原作となった、ライマン・フランク・ボーム（Lyman Frank Baum /bɔːm/）が 1900 年に発表した児童文学小説『オズの魔法使い』（The Wonderful Wizard of Oz）が採用され、原作と映画の違いが考察できる内容となっている。（原作と映画のタイトルの違いは "Wonderful" の有無である。）また、映画が制作された時代背景や「虹の彼方に」が伝えるメッセージに関するエッセイなども収録され、この映画に対する理解をいっそう深められるようになっている。

　映画『オズの魔法使』の大きな特徴の一つは、冒頭とラストシーンはモノクロフィルムで撮影されているのに対して、ドロシーが竜巻に巻き込まれ飛ばされたオズの国のパートは、当時はまだ珍しかったカラーフィルムで撮影されていることである。オズの国の華やかな描写がきわめて印象的である。本書は、映画の世界観をそのまま味わっていただくために、「名作映画で TOEIC®」シリーズではじめて、カラー印刷を採用した。

　『オズの魔法使』を題材とした TOEIC 教材を作成するにあたっては、これまでの経験や知見を活かし、執筆者で議論と検討を重ねた。本書がみなさんの英語力の総合的な向上のお役にたてれば幸いである。

　本書の出版に際しても、英宝社編集部の下村幸一氏と販売部の橋本稔寛氏には終始適切なご助言とご支援をいただいた。改めて感謝の意を表したい。

2019 年 8 月

著者一同

目　次

Aᴄᴛ 1 On the Kansas Prairies

 0:00:00-0:08:00

Words & Phrases

次の英単語・フレーズの意味を、下記の語群より選びなさい。　　　🔟 02

1. be occupied with . . .	( )	6. incubator	( )	11. prairie	( )
2. cellar	( )	7. innocent	( )	12. release	( )
3. chase	( )	8. lumber	( )	13. tightly	( )
4. cupboard	( )	9. philosophy	( )	14. trap-door	( )
5. dedicate	( )	10. plow	( )	15. wander	( )

a. 〜で忙しい	d. 材木	g. しっかりと	j. 耕す	m. 哲学
b. 追いかける	e. 捧げる	h. 食器棚	k. 孵化器	n. 跳ね上げ戸
c. （映画の）公開	f. さまよう	i. 大草原	l. 地下室	o. 無邪気な

Listening Tips

英語のリズム

　英語を正しく読んだり書いたりできるようになるために「英文法」の知識が必要なのと同様に、英語を正しく聞き取れるようになるためにも、いわば「英音法」とでも呼ぶべき、英語の音声に関する知識が不可欠です。英音法の知識があれば、リスニングだけではなくスピーキングも上達します。Listening Tips では、英語の音声に関するさまざまなトピックを学びます。

　最初に学ぶのは、英語のリズムです。英語のリズムの特徴は、強く読まれる語と弱く読まれる語が（比較的）規則的に繰り返し現れる強勢拍リズムであるということです。基本的に、名詞・動詞・形容詞・副詞などの内容語 (content word) は強く・長く発音されるのに対して、冠詞・人称代名詞・助動詞・関係詞・前置詞・接続詞などの機能語 (function word) は弱く・短く発音されます。

Exercises ─────────────────── 🔟 03 🆂 02

内容語と機能語の区別に注意して次の台詞を音読しましょう。

1. She isn't coming yet, Toto. Did she hurt you? She tried to, didn't she?

2. Aunt Em, just listen to what Miss Gulch did to Toto!

3. Zeke, what am I going to do about Miss Gulch?

Part 1 写真の場面を最も適切に表している音声を選びなさい。 🎧 04 Ⓢ 03

1. Ⓐ Ⓑ Ⓒ Ⓓ

Part 2 問いかけに対する最も適切な応答を選びなさい。 🎧05-06 Ⓢ 04-05

 遊んでいたドロシーが豚小屋に落ちて大騒ぎ。ハンクとジークが助けて事なきを得るが、エムおばさん（エム・ゲール）がやってきて……

2. Ⓐ Ⓑ Ⓒ

 2に続く場面。ハンクとジークはエムおばさんたちに雇われているので、農場の仕事をしなければならないのだ。

3. Ⓐ Ⓑ Ⓒ

Part 3 会話を聞き、設問に答えなさい。 🎧 07 Ⓢ 06
（登場話者：Dorothy, Zeke, Hunk）

 ドロシーは自分が抱えている問題について、農場で働いているハンクとジークがアドバイスをしてくれないかと考えているようだが…

4. What is Dorothy's problem?
   (A) Miss Gulch's cat always chases Toto.
   (B) She is in trouble with Miss Gulch.
   (C) She cannot take care of her own dog.
   (D) Hunk is too busy to listen to her.

5. Why is Zeke unable to help Dorothy?
  (A) He is occupied with his work.
  (B) He is indifferent to her.
  (C) He has been brainwashed by Miss Gulch.
  (D) He has to go into the garden immediately.

6. What is Hunk's advice?
  (A) Dorothy should never come home.
  (B) Dorothy should come home using another route.
  (C) Dorothy should come home at a different time of day.
  (D) Dorothy should not come home with Miss Gulch.

Part 4 ナレーションを聞き、設問に答えなさい。 08 ⑤ 07

 映画の冒頭に表示される献辞（制作者からの感謝を込めたメッセージ）を聞いて
みよう。右のイラストは、原作の著作権表記の挿絵である。

7. Look at the illustration. What is most likely the release year of this film?
  (A) 1859
  (B) 1899
  (C) 1913
  (D) 1939

8. What does the narrator say about the original story?
  (A) It is difficult to understand.
  (B) It is old-fashioned.
  (C) It has attracted many people for decades.
  (D) It is based on a famous folk tale.

9. To whom is this film dedicated?
  (A) All youngsters and children
  (B) Only grown-ups and the elderly
  (C) Fans of the story and the pure of heart
  (D) Ladies and gentlemen

音声を聞き、適切な語句を空所に書き入れなさい。

Part 1

Ⅱ 04   Ⓢ 03

1. (A) The girl and the dog are looking at (^{1}) (^{2}).

   (B) The girl and the dog are (^{3}) in the woods.

   (C) The girl is holding her dog (^{4}) in her arms.

   (D) There are no (^{5}) in the sky.

Part 2

Ⅱ 05-06   Ⓢ 04-05

2. Now, you and Hunk get back to that (^{1})!

   (A) (^{2}) (^{3}), Mrs. Gale.

   (B) (^{4}) you are.

   (C) Are you all right?

3. Have some (^{5}). Just (^{6}).

   (A) Thanks.

   (B) There must be.

   (C) (^{7}) (^{8}) easy.

Part 3

Dorothy: Zeke, what am I going to (^{1}) (^{2}) Miss Gulch? Just

because Toto chases her old cat . . .

Zeke: Listen, honey, I've (^{3}) (^{4}) get these (^{5}) to

get in.

Hunk: Now look, Dorothy, you aren't using your head about Miss Gulch.

You'd think you didn't have any brains at all.

Dorothy: Hunk, I have (^{6}) (^{7}) brains!

Hunk: Well, why don't you use them? When you come home, don't go by

Miss Gulch's (^{8}). Then Toto won't get in her garden and

you won't get (^{9}) (^{10}) (^{11}). See?

Part 4

For nearly (^{1}) (^{2}) this story has given faithful service to the

Young in Heart; and Time has been (^{3}) to put its kindly philosophy

(^{4}) (^{5}) (^{6}). To those of you who have been faithful to

it in return, and to the Young in Heart, we (^{7}) this picture.

10. This old incubator has _____ bad.
    (A) gone
    (B) come
    (C) changed
    (D) fallen

11. Miss Gulch hit Toto on _____ back with a rake.
    (A) it's
    (B) my
    (C) a
    (D) the

12. Dorothy, use your head; your head is not made _____ straw, you know.
    (A) of
    (B) by
    (C) for
    (D) in

13. Now, Dorothy, stop _____ things.
    (A) imagine
    (B) imagined
    (C) imagining
    (D) imagination

14. Now, you just help us out today and find _____ a place where you will not get into any trouble.
    (A) you
    (B) your
    (C) you're
    (D) yourself

　エムおばさんたちは忙しくて、ドロシーの問題に耳を貸してくれそうもない。ドロシーは自分の今の気持ちを歌う。(♪ 「虹の彼方に」)

Somewhere over the rainbow
Way up high
There's a land that I heard of
Once in a lullaby

Somewhere over the rainbow
Skies are blue
And the dreams ---15--- you dare to dream
Really do ---16--- true

Someday I'll wish upon a star
And wake up where the clouds are far behind me
Where troubles melt ---17--- lemon drops
Away above the chimney tops
That's ---18--- you'll find me

15. (A) that
　　(B) where
　　(C) as
　　(D) what

16. (A) come
　　(B) become
　　(C) realize
　　(D) get

17. (A) similar to
　　(B) like
　　(C) the same
　　(D) as if

18. (A) what
　　(B) when
　　(C) where
　　(D) there

この Act で扱う映画の場面は、原作とは異なる映画のオリジナルである。原作ではドロシーたちの生活はどう描かれているだろうか。

Dorothy lived in the midst of the great Kansas prairies, with Uncle Henry, who was a farmer, and Aunt Em, who was the farmer's wife. Their house was small, for the lumber to build it had to be carried by wagon many miles. There were four walls, a floor and a roof, which made one room; and this room contained a rusty looking cooking stove, a cupboard for the dishes, a table, three or four chairs, and the beds. Uncle Henry and Aunt Em had a big bed in one corner, and Dorothy a little bed in another corner. There was no garret at all, and no cellar — except a small hole dug in the ground, called a cyclone cellar, where the family could go in case one of those great whirlwinds arose, mighty enough to crush any building in its path. It was reached by a trap-door in the middle of the floor, from which a ladder led down into the small, dark hole.

When Dorothy stood in the doorway and looked around, she could see nothing but the great gray prairie on every side. Not a tree nor a house broke the broad sweep of flat country that reached to the edge of the sky in all directions. The sun had baked the plowed land into a gray mass, with little cracks running through it. Even the grass was not green, for the sun had burned the tops of the long blades until they were the same gray color to be seen everywhere. Once the house had been painted, but the sun blistered the paint and the rains washed it away, and now the house was as dull and gray as everything else.

19. Why is Henry and Em's house so small?
    (A) There weren't enough farmers in the prairies.
    (B) There wasn't much room for a new house in Kansas.
    (C) There wasn't enough wood nearby.
    (D) They had to save money to make a cyclone cellar.

20. What is NOT found in the house?
    (A) Two beds
    (B) A few chairs
    (C) Cooking equipment
    (D) An attic

21. What will they have to do if a cyclone hits the area?
    (A) Evacuate to a small hole dug in the garden.
    (B) Climb up a ladder to the roof to follow the cyclone's path.
    (C) Rescue their neighbors trapped in buildings.
    (D) Go down to the basement built for such emergencies.

22. What can be seen from the house?
    (A) Barren desert without any trees
    (B) Broad roads going in various directions
    (C) Beautiful countryside dotted with houses and barns
    (D) Flat land that is dry because of the weather

23. What can be inferred from the passage?
    (A) The house is not newly built.
    (B) Dorothy feels lonely because she does not have any friends.
    (C) No crops will grow due to a lack of water.
    (D) Dorothy suffers from malnutrition.

品詞（1）

　英語の文を正しく理解するためには、文中の語・句・節が、それぞれ、文のどの基本要素（主語・目的語・補語）の働きをしているかを正確に見分ける必要があります。その際、重要になるのが品詞という概念です。単語は、その形や意味、働きによって名詞・動詞・形容詞・副詞・前置詞などの品詞に分けられます。それぞれの品詞はそれぞれ異なった機能を持っていて、その機能によって、どの語とどの語が結びつくのか、または結びつかないのかが決まってくるのです。品詞を意識するようになると、どの語の集まりが文のどの基本要素として機能しているかを理解しやすくなります。

品詞とその機能

種　類	機　　能
名　詞	人や事物の名前や概念を表す。主語、目的語、補語になる。例：girl, movie
動　詞	動作や状態を表し、時制や主語の人称などによって語形を変える。例：eat, belong
形容詞	人や事物の性質などを表す。補語や、名詞の修飾語になる。例：beautiful, ugly
副　詞	時や場所などを表し、動詞、形容詞、他の副詞や文全体を修飾する。例：very, so
代名詞	名詞の代わりに用いられる。例：he, she, it
冠　詞	名詞の前に置かれ、その名詞が特定できるかどうかを示す。例：a, an, the
助動詞	動詞の前に置かれ、その動詞と結びついて可能・義務などの意味を示す。例：can
前置詞	名詞の前に置かれ、後ろの名詞とともに形容詞句や副詞句の役割を果たす。例：at
接続詞	語と語、句と句、節と節を結びつける。例：and, but, or, so
間投詞	話し手の感情を表したり、呼びかけに使われたりする。例：oh, alas

Exercises

(　　　) 内から適切な語句を選びましょう。

1. The history of our (civilized / civilization) is the theme of his new book.

2. She is such a (considerate / consideration) person that everyone loves her.

3. (Patience / Patient) is bitter, but its fruit is sweet.

4. Sorry, the site is (temporary / temporarily) closed; please come back later.

5. (Success / Successful) is not final, failure is not fatal: it is the courage to continue that counts.

Aᴄᴛ 2 Running Away

 0:08:00-0:15:04

Words & Phrases

次の英単語・フレーズの意味を、下記の語群より選びなさい。　　🅣 12

1. authentic	( )	6. cradle	( )	11. infinite	( )
2. barn	( )	7. creep	( )	12. menace	( )
3. carefree	( )	8. crystal	( )	13. polka-dot	( )
4. careworn	( )	9. drag	( )	14. rock	( )
5. chronic	( )	10. gaze	( )	15. worn-out	( )

a. 脅威　　　　　d. 水晶　　　　　g. のんきな　　　j. 水玉模様の　　m. やつれた
b. じっと見る　　e. すりきれた　　h. 這う　　　　　k. 慢性の　　　　n. 揺らす
c. 真正の　　　　f. 納屋　　　　　i. 引きずる　　　l. 無限の　　　　o. ゆりかご

Listening Tips

機能語とあいまい母音

　内容語は強く長く、はっきりと発音されるために聞き取りは難しくありませんが、機能語は弱く短く発音されるために、その分、聞き取ることは困難です。日本の学校英語教育では、英文を読む際に、単語を強く読むように指導されることはあっても、弱く短く読む単語があることは指導されないのが一般的ですが、弱く短い部分があってはじめて、英語の強勢拍リズムが生まれます。機能語を内容語のように強く長く発音しないように十分に注意しましょう。

　Exercises の問題 2 の助動詞 can について、多くの英語学習者は「キャン」/kæn/ と発音されると思っていますが、機能語である can はほとんどの場合、弱く短く /kən/ と発音されます。問題 3 の could も「クッド」/kʊd/ ではなく、弱く短い /kəd/ です。can と could には /ə/ という記号で表されるあいまい母音 (schwa) が含まれることに気をつけましょう。

Exercises ━━━━━━━━━━━━━━━━━━━━━━ 🅣 13 Ⓢ 08

次の台詞の（　　　）内の語を聞き取り、全文を音読しましょう。

1. (　　　　) didn't know (　　　) (　　　　　) doing anything wrong.

2. (　　　　) (　　　　) send (　　　　) (　　　) bed (　　　　　) supper.

3. Why, it's just like (　　　) (　　　　　) read what was inside (　　　) (　　　　).

Part 1 写真の場面を最も適切に表している音声を選びなさい。 🎬 14 Ⓢ 09

1. Ⓐ Ⓑ Ⓒ Ⓓ

Part 2 問いかけに対する最も適切な応答を選びなさい。 🎬 15-16 Ⓢ 10-11

 ガルチさんが血相を変えてドロシーたちの家にやってきた。ガルチさんは家から出てきたヘンリーおじさんに…

2. Ⓐ Ⓑ Ⓒ

 家出中のドロシーは、占い師のマーヴェル教授の馬車を見つける。水晶玉をのぞきこんだ教授は、そこに女性が見えるという。ドロシーは…

3. Ⓐ Ⓑ Ⓒ

Part 3 会話を聞き、設問に答えなさい。 🎬 17 Ⓢ 12
（登場話者：Miss Gulch, Uncle Henry, Dorothy）

 Part 2 の 2 に続く場面。ガルチさんはドロシーの飼犬トトのことで何か問題を抱えているようだ。

4. What is the problem?
   (A) Dorothy bit Miss Gulch.
   (B) Dorothy bit her own dog.
   (C) Dorothy's dog bit Miss Gulch.
   (D) Dorothy's dog bit Dorothy.

5. What does Miss Gulch want to do?
   (A) Bring the dog to the Sheriff
   (B) Have a community meeting
   (C) Destroy the dog's kennel completely
   (D) Treat her injured leg

6. Why does Uncle Henry say, "Will we, Em?"
   (A) He is trying to calm down Miss Gulch.
   (B) He would like an explanation.
   (C) He is angry with Em.
   (D) He wants Em to agree with him.

Part 4 マーヴェル教授の話を聞き、設問に答えなさい。　 18　 13

> ドロシーに、一緒に旅に連れて行って欲しいと頼まれたマーヴェル教授は、まず
> 水晶玉を見てみようという。教授がそこに見たものは…

7. What does Professor Marvel talk about first?
   (A) A burning house
   (B) A horse jumping over a fence
   (C) Two buildings
   (D) A crystal-clear sea

8. What does he say the woman in the crystal ball is wearing?
   (A) Running shoes
   (B) Worn-out pants
   (C) A dotted dress
   (D) A weather-proof jacket

9. According to him, what is true about the woman?
   (A) She is having a heart attack.
   (B) She is happy and carefree.
   (C) She is suffering from a chronic disease.
   (D) She is in deep sorrow.

Dictation

音声を聞き、適切な語句を空所に書き入れなさい。

Part 1

🄣 14　Ⓢ 09

1. (A) Dorothy is (¹　　　　　) with her eyes wide open.

   (B) The man is looking at something in his (²　　　　　) hand.

   (C) There are many (³　　　　　) in the room.

   (D) There is a (⁴　　　　　) on the man's (⁵　　　　　).

Part 2

🄣 15-16　Ⓢ 10-11

2. I want to see you and your wife (¹　　　　　) (²　　　　　), about Dorothy.

   (A) How do you do, Dorothy.

   (B) Well, what has she (³　　　　　)?

   (C) Of course, we (⁴　　　　　).

3. What's the woman you see in the (⁵　　　　　) doing?

   (A) Her name is (⁶　　　　　).

   (B) No, (⁷　　　　　) (⁸　　　　　) me.

   (C) Well, I can't (⁹　　　　　) (¹⁰　　　　　).

Part 3

Miss Gulch: Don't you know what Dorothy has done? I'm all (^{1})

(^{2}) from the (^{3}) on my leg!

Uncle Henry: You (^{4}) she (^{5}) you?

Miss Gulch: No, her dog!

Uncle Henry: Oh, she (^{6}) her dog, eh?

Miss Gulch: No! That dog is a (^{7}) to the community. I'm taking

him to the (^{8}) and make sure he's (^{9}).

Dorothy: (^{10})? Toto? Oh, you can't! You (^{11})!

Auntie Em! Uncle Henry! You won't let her, will you?

Uncle Henry: Of course, we won't. Will we, Em?

Part 4

Now you can open your eyes. We'll (^{1}) (^{2}) the crystal. Ah,

what's this I see? A house with a (^{3}) (^{4}), and a (^{5})

with a (^{6}) (^{7}) of a running horse. There's a woman. She's

wearing a polka-dot dress. Her face is (^{8}). She's crying; someone

has (^{9}) her. Someone has just about broken her (^{10}).

10. There is a law _____ folks against dogs that bite.
    (A) protecting
    (B) protects
    (C) protected
    (D) protection

11. Well, that is _____ the Sheriff to decide.
    (A) of
    (B) for
    (C) what
    (D) whether

12. Here is his order allowing me _____ him.
    (A) take
    (B) took
    (C) taking
    (D) to take

13. _____ poor Toto will have to go.
    (A) I wish
    (B) If only
    (C) I'm afraid
    (D) I'm concerned about

14. They will be coming back for you _____ a minute.
    (A) in
    (B) by
    (C) for
    (D) to

Part 4 の少し前の場面。マーヴェル教授はドロシーに、これから占いに使う水晶玉がどのようなものなのかを説明している。

This is the same genuine, magic, authentic crystal ---15--- by the priests of Isis and Osiris in the days of the Pharaohs of Egypt, ---16--- Cleopatra first saw the approach of Julius Caesar and Mark Antony and so on. Now, you had better ---17--- your eyes, my child, for a moment, in order to be better in tune with the infinite; we can't do these things ---18--- reaching out into the infinite.

15. (A) use
    (B) used
    (C) using
    (D) to use

16. (A) to whom
    (B) in which
    (C) of that
    (D) what

17. (A) close
    (B) closed
    (C) closing
    (D) to close

18. (A) except
    (B) without
    (C) but
    (D) beyond

ドロシーは家ごと竜巻に巻き込まれてしまうのだが、原作ではこの場面
はどのように描写されているだろうか。

A strange thing then happened.

The house whirled around two or three times and rose slowly through the air. Dorothy felt as if she were going up in a balloon.

The north and south winds met where the house stood, and made it the exact center of the cyclone. —[1]—. In the middle of a cyclone the air is generally still, but the great pressure of the wind on every side of the house raised it up higher and higher, until it was at the very top of the cyclone; and there it remained and was carried miles and miles away as easily as you could carry a feather.

It was very dark, and the wind howled horribly around her, but Dorothy found she was riding quite easily. —[2]—. After the first few whirls around, and one other time when the house tipped badly, she felt as if she were being rocked gently, like a baby in a cradle.

—[3]—. He ran about the room, now here, now there, barking loudly; but Dorothy sat quite still on the floor and waited to see what would happen.

Once Toto got too near the open trap-door, and fell in; and at first the little girl thought she had lost him. —[4]—. But soon she saw one of his ears sticking up through the hole, for the strong pressure of the air was keeping him up so that he could not fall. She crept to the hole, caught Toto by the ear, and dragged him into the room again; afterward closing the trap-door so that no more accidents could happen.

19. What is the strange thing that happened?
    (A) The house moved up and down several times.
    (B) A balloon carried by the wind hit the house.
    (C) The cyclone blew the house to the north, then to the south.
    (D) The house was lifted upward into the sky.

20. According to the passage, what is true about the house?
    (A) It was continuously shaken badly by strong winds.
    (B) It remained tilted while it was carried far away.
    (C) It did not move at all as it was built solidly.
    (D) It was lifted to the very top of the cyclone.

21. In the passage, the word "rocked" in paragraph 4, line 4, is closest in meaning
    to
    (A) moved softly back and forth
    (B) built of hard stone
    (C) sung a lullaby
    (D) kept in a small space

22. Why did Toto survive the incident?
    (A) He was able to escape from the open trap-door.
    (B) The trap-door was too small for him.
    (C) The wind was so strong that it held him up.
    (D) His ear was trapped in the door.

23. In which of the positions marked [1], [2], [3] and [4] does the following sentence best belong?
    "Toto didn't like it."
    (A) [1]
    (B) [2]
    (C) [3]
    (D) [4]

　ある単語がどの品詞であるかは、その語尾を見れば、おおよその見当がつきます。construct（建設する）という動詞に -ion という接尾辞を付け加えることによって、construction（建設）という名詞になります。また、接尾辞 -ive を付け加えることによって、constructive（建設的な）という形容詞になり、さらに接尾辞 -ly を付け加えることによって、constructively（建設的に）という副詞になります。次の表で、さまざまな品詞を作る接尾辞および接頭辞を確認するとともに、接尾辞（接頭辞）がつく前の単語の形と意味を考えましょう。

主な接尾辞・接頭辞

動詞を作る接尾辞・接頭辞					
-ize	specialize	「専攻する」	**-ify**	purify	「浄化する」
-en	blacken	「黒くする」	**en-**	enlarge	「大きくする」
形容詞を作る接尾辞					
-al	natural	「自然な」	**-ive**	attractive	「魅力的な」
-ful	beautiful	「美しい」	**-ous**	dangerous	「危険な」
-ic	academic	「学問の」	**-able**	washable	「洗える」
名詞を作る接尾辞					
-(at)ion	organization	「組織」	**-ment**	establishment	「設立」
-ance	appearance	「出現」	**-er**	employer	「雇用者」
-ity	productivity	「生産性」	**-ness**	happiness	「幸福」

Exercises

（　　　）内から適切な語句を選びましょう。

1. (Beauty / Beautiful) lies in the eye of the beholder.

2. The sculpture *Laocoön* is famous as an artistic (express / expression) of pain and agony.

3. If you want to be a good scientist, you must be (imaginary / imaginative).

4. Scientists said it was really difficult to (species / specify) the cause of the bridge collapse.

5. Poor (manage / management) can sometimes lead to business failure.

Act 3 Over the Rainbow

 0:15:04-0:24:51

Words & Phrases

次の英単語・フレーズの意味を、下記の語群より選びなさい。　　　　　⑪ 22

1. breathe	( )	6. fertile	( )	11. muddle	( )
2. brook	( )	7. heroine	( )	12. national	( )
3. chuckle	( )	8. infer	( )	13. teller	( )
4. demolish	( )	9. marvellous	( )	14. ugly	( )
5. evil	( )	10. miracle	( )	15. windowpane	( )

a. 息をする　　d. 金銭出納係　　g. 混乱させる　　j. すばらしい　　m. ヒロイン
b. 小川　　　　e. くすくす笑う　h. 邪悪な　　　　k. 破壊する　　　n. 窓ガラス
c. 奇跡　　　　f. 国の　　　　　i. 推測する　　　l. 肥沃な　　　　o. 醜い

Listening Tips

強形と弱形

　Act 2 の Listening Tips では、通常、助動詞 can は /kæn/ ではなく、弱く短く /kən/ と発音されること、また、/ə/ をあいまい母音と呼ぶことを学びました。

　一般的な英和辞典で can の発音を調べると、/k(ə)n, 《強》kæn/ のように表記されています。《強》は強形を表します。can が文末に生起した場合や特に意味を強める場合、また not が付いた否定縮約形 can't では、強形の /kæn/ や /kænt/ となりますが、その他の多くの場合、can は弱形の /k(ə)n/ で発音されます。同様に、will や would も強形の /wɪl/ や /wʊd/ ではなく、弱形の /w(ə)l, (ə)l/ や /wəd, əd/ で発音される場合がほとんどです。さらに、at /ət, æt/, for /fər, fɔːr/, from /frəm, frʌm/, to /tə, tuː/ などの前置詞にも弱形と強形があり、ほとんどの場合、弱形で発音されます。強形の発音しか知らないと、弱形で発音された語をまったく理解することができませんので、弱形と強形の二通りの発音がある場合のあることを忘れないようにしましょう。

Exercises ──────────────── ⑪ 23 ⓢ 14

あいまい母音を含む（　　　　　　）内の語を聞き取り、台詞を音読しましょう。

1. We can't look (　　　　) her now.

2. The Munchkins are happy because you (　　　　　) freed (　　　　) (　　　　) the Wicked Witch of the East.

Part 1 写真の場面を最も適切に表している音声を選びなさい。　🎧 24　Ⓢ 15

1. Ⓐ Ⓑ Ⓒ Ⓓ

Part 2 問いかけに対する最も適切な応答を選びなさい。　🎧 25-26　Ⓢ 16-17

竜巻に巻き込まれたドロシーとトト。ようやく地上に降りて外に出てみると、不思議な女性が現れる。女性はドロシーに…

2. Ⓐ Ⓑ Ⓒ

どうやら竜巻にとばされた先はカンザスではないらしい。女性の話の中にでてくるなぞめいた言葉について、ドロシーは疑問をぶつける。

3. Ⓐ Ⓑ Ⓒ

Part 3 会話を聞き、設問に答えなさい。　🎧 27　Ⓢ 18
　　　　　（登場話者：Glinda, Dorothy）

Part 2の2に続く場面。突然空から降ってきたドロシーに、グリンダはいろいろと質問をしているのだが、お互い話がかみあわず…

4. What do the Munchkins want to know about Dorothy?
   (A) Whether she is evil or not
   (B) Where she was born
   (C) What she wants to do
   (D) How old she is

5. What does Dorothy mean when she says "I beg your pardon"?
   (A) She wants to hear Glinda's words again.
   (B) She notices she has been impolite to Glinda.
   (C) She is angry and wants to stop talking.
   (D) She wants Glinda to give her some time to think.

6. What can be inferred about Glinda?
   (A) She is old and ugly.
   (B) She is a bad witch.
   (C) She is a good witch.
   (D) She is a Munchkin.

Part 4 グリンダの話を聞き、設問に答えなさい。　⓫ 28　Ⓢ 19

グリンダはドロシーに自分たちの疑問を伝える。ドロシーたちの到来が引き起こ
した、とある「事件」が原因なのだが、それは…

7. Why did Glinda come here?
   (A) To see what had happened
   (B) To find a new residence
   (C) To pray for the victim
   (D) To rescue the bad witch

8. What does Glinda seem to think about Dorothy?
   (A) She is nothing but a tiny little girl.
   (B) She is a new witch in their land.
   (C) She is a bad girl who could harm the
       Munchkins.
   (D) She is a poor girl who has lost her home.

9. Look at the illustration. What does Glinda refer to
   when she says "that's all that's left of the Wicked
   Witch of the East"?
   (A) A house
   (B) A pair of shoes
   (C) A windowpane
   (D) A dog

Dictation

音声を聞き、適切な語句を空所に書き入れなさい。

Part 1

T1 24　S 15

1. (A) Dorothy is looking (^{1}　　　　) (^{2}　　　) her dog.

　(B) Toto is (^{3}　　　　) his (^{4}　　　　) into Dorothy's (^{5}　　　　).

　(C) Dorothy is looking at something (^{6}　　　) (^{7}　　　) (^{8}　　　).

　(D) Dorothy is (^{9}　　　) (^{10}　　　) her basket.

Part 2

T1 25-26　S 16-17

2. Well, is that the (^{1}　　　　)?

　(A) Who, Toto? Toto's my dog.

　(B) I'm not a (^{2}　　　) at all.

　(C) (^{3}　　　) way do we go?

3. If you (^{4}　　　), what are Munchkins?

　(A) It's Munchkinland, and you are their (^{5}　　　　) (^{6}　　　　).

　(B) The Munchkins are very happy because you have (^{7}　　　) (^{8}　　　).

　(C) They're the little people who (^{9}　　　) (^{10}　　　) this land.

Part 3

Glinda: So what the Munchkins want to know is — Are you a (^{1})

witch or a (^{2}) witch?

Dorothy: But I've already told you, I'm not a witch (^{3}) (^{4}).

Witches are (^{5}) and (^{6}).

Munchkins: [*Chuckles*]

Dorothy: What was that?

Glinda: The Munchkins. They're laughing because I *am* a witch. I'm

Glinda, the Witch of the (^{7}).

Dorothy: You are! Oh, I (^{8}) (^{9}) (^{10})! But I've

never heard of a (^{11}) witch before.

Glinda: Only bad witches are (^{12}).

Part 4

Well, I'm a little (^{1}). The Munchkins called me because a new

witch has just (^{2}) (^{3}) (^{4}) on the Wicked Witch of

the (^{5}). And there's the house, and (^{6}) (^{7}) (^{8}),

and that's (^{9}) (^{10}) (^{11}) of the Wicked Witch of the East.

10. Toto, I have a feeling we are not in Kansas
   _____ more.
   (A) no
   (B) still
   (C) any
   (D) some

11. It really was no miracle. _____ happened
   was just this.
   (A) That
   (B) What
   (C) It
   (D) Such

12. Just then, the witch went _____ off on
   her broomstick.
   (A) fly
   (B) flew
   (C) fled
   (D) flying

13. The house landed on the Wicked Witch,
   _____ was not a healthy situation for her.
   (A) witch
   (B) which
   (C) that
   (D) who

14. We thank you very sweetly _____ doing it
   so neatly.
   (A) for
   (B) of
   (C) on
   (D) with

 ドロシーが悪い魔女ではないとわかったので、グリンダはマンチキンたちに出てくるようにと呼びかける。(♪「みんな出てらっしゃい」)

Come out, come out, ---15--- you are

And meet the young lady, ---16--- fell from a star

She fell from the sky, she fell very far

And Kansas, she says, ---17--- the name of the star

She ---18--- you good news

Or haven't you heard?

When she fell out of Kansas, a miracle occurred

15. (A) where
    (B) wherever
    (C) anywhere
    (D) whatever

16. (A) who
    (B) what
    (C) whom
    (D) whose

17. (A) is
    (B) to be
    (C) are
    (D) been

18. (A) introduces
    (B) explains
    (C) takes
    (D) brings

家ごと竜巻に巻き込まれたドロシーが目を覚まして外に出てみると、そこは別世界だった。原作の描写を鑑賞しよう。

She was awakened by a shock, so sudden and severe that if Dorothy had not been lying on the soft bed she might have been hurt. As it was, the jar made her catch her breath and wonder what had happened; and Toto put his cold little nose into her face and whined dismally. Dorothy sat up and noticed that the house was not moving; nor was it dark, for the bright sunshine came in at the window, flooding the little room. She sprang from her bed and with Toto at her heels ran and opened the door.

The little girl gave a cry of amazement and looked about her, her eyes growing bigger and bigger at the wonderful sights she saw.

The cyclone had set the house down, very gently — for a cyclone — in the midst of a country of marvelous beauty. There were lovely patches of green sward all about, with stately trees bearing rich and luscious fruits. Banks of gorgeous flowers were on every hand, and birds with rare and brilliant plumage sang and fluttered in the trees and bushes. A little way off was a small brook, rushing and sparkling along between green banks, and murmuring in a voice very grateful to a little girl who had lived so long on the dry, gray prairies.

Notes:

jar「衝撃」whine「(犬が) 鳴く」dismally「みじめに」sward「芝生、草地」luscious「おいしそうな」plumage「羽毛」flutter「羽ばたいて飛ぶ」

19. Why was Dorothy able to survive the house falling?
   (A) The mattress protected her from injury.
   (B) Toto guided her to a safe place.
   (C) She stopped breathing to prepare for the impact.
   (D) The house was built on a hard surface.

20. What did Dorothy notice when she woke up?
   (A) The floor was flooded with water.
   (B) The house was not shaking any longer.
   (C) It was dark and she could not see well.
   (D) Toto had brought her slippers to the bedside.

21. How did Dorothy feel when she opened the door?
   (A) She was filled with grief and began to weep.
   (B) She was shocked as the cyclone had demolished everything.
   (C) She wondered if she could ever get back home again.
   (D) She was fascinated by the marvelous scenery.

22. Which is true about the cyclone?
   (A) It changed the gray prairie into fertile green pasture.
   (B) It damaged the beautiful countryside.
   (C) It blew the house upside down into a valley.
   (D) It brought Dorothy to a heavenly place.

23. What is NOT seen in the new land?
   (A) A babbling stream
   (B) Trees full of fruit
   (C) Uncommon birds
   (D) Automated teller machines

動詞と文型

1. A miracle occurred.	(S + V)	第 1 文型
2. Toto is my dog.	(S + V + C)	第 2 文型
3. We thank you very sweetly.	(S + V + O)	第 3 文型
4. She brings you good news.	(S + V + O + O)	第 4 文型
5. I let Toto go in her garden.	(S + V + O + C)	第 5 文型

　動詞の種類にしたがって、英文の形式を 5 つに分類することができます。これを 5 文型といいます。

5 文型とそれぞれの機能

文　型	機　　能
第 1 文型	Birds sing. のように、動詞 sing の働きは他に及ばない（自動詞）。
第 2 文型	He is a scholar. のように、動詞 is の働きは他に及ばないが、補語 a scholar がなければ完全な意味を表せない（不完全自動詞）。
第 3 文型	The girl picked some flowers. のように、動詞 picked の動作は目的語 flowers に及ぶ（他動詞）。
第 4 文型	He gave me a watch. のように、2 つの目的語 me, a watch を必要とする（授与動詞）。give, send, tell, teach など。
第 5 文型	He made her happy. のように、動詞 made の働きが目的語 her に及ぶが、目的語のほかに補語 happy がなければ完全な意味を表せない（不完全他動詞）。

Exercises

(　　　) 内から適切な語句を選びましょう。

1. You look pale; why don't you (lie / lay) down and rest for a while?

2. He (laid / lied) the book open on the table and walked away.

3. I sent (Mary a birthday gift / a birthday gift Mary).

4. No one can (force / make) you to love.

5. You are not (admitted / allowed) to use your smartphone in this classroom.

ACT 4 Start at the Beginning

 0:24:51-0:32:42

Words & Phrases

次の英単語・フレーズの意味を、下記の語群より選びなさい。 🎧 32

1. absolutely	( )	6. direction	( )	11. phenomenon	( )
2. altogether	( )	7. drought	( )	12. reliably	( )
3. at the mercy of	( )	8. legally	( )	13. soil	( )
4. border	( )	9. mortgage	( )	14. undeniably	( )
5. broomstick	( )	10. palace	( )	15. wand	( )

a. 確実に　　　　　d. 宮殿　　g. 合法的に　　j. 杖　　m. ～のなすがままに
b. 完全に、全体で　e. 境界　　h. 住宅ローン　k. 土壌　n. ほうきの柄
c. 干ばつ　　　　　f. 現象　　i. 絶対に　　　l. 方向　o. まぎれもなく

Listening Tips

連結

　連結 (linking) とはその名の通り、in an hour（一時間で）や an apple のように、前の単語の最後の子音と次の単語の最初の母音がつながって発音される現象のことです。ちなみに、in の子音 /n/ は、本来、舌先が歯茎に接触して発音される歯茎鼻音と呼ばれる音ですが、多くの日本人英語学習者は、この語末の /n/ を、誤って日本語の「うどん」「ペン」などの語における語末の「ン」を使って発音してしまい、次の母音に繋げて読むことができません。in an hour のような n 連結をうまく発音するためには、/n/ を発音するときに舌先をしっかりと歯茎に付けるよう意識することです。また、an apple は、/ən/ + /æpl̩/ であるというよりは、/ə/ + /næpl̩/ であるというつもりでいた方が、発音も聞き取りも楽になるでしょう。連結は /n/ 以外の子音でも起こります。

Exercises ──────────── 🎧 33 Ⓢ 20

次の台詞の（　　　　　）内を聞き取り、連結に注意して全文を音読しましょう。

1. It (　　　) (　　　) (　　　　　). I didn't mean to (　　　) (　　　　　).

2. Be gone before somebody (　　　) (　　) (　　　　) (　　) you, too!

3. I'd (　　　) (　　　　) to (　　) (　　) (　　) (　　　) Oz altogether, but,
　 (　　　) (　　) the way back to Kansas?

4. (　　　) (　　　　) best to (　　　) (　　　) the beginning.

Part 1　写真の場面を最も適切に表している音声を選びなさい。　🎧 34　Ⓢ 21

1. Ⓐ Ⓑ Ⓒ Ⓓ

Part 2　問いかけに対する最も適切な応答を選びなさい。　🎧 35-36　Ⓢ 22-23

 東の悪い魔女が死んだことでマンチキンたちが大喜びしているところへ、突然西の悪い魔女が煙とともに現れる。彼女は…

2. Ⓐ Ⓑ Ⓒ

 Part 3 に続く場面。グリンダはまだ、ドロシーのことを超自然的な力を持つ「良い魔女」だと思っているらしい。

3. Ⓐ Ⓑ Ⓒ

Part 3　会話を聞き、設問に答えなさい。　🎧 37　Ⓢ 24
　　　　（登場話者：Glinda, Dorothy）

 Part 6 に続く場面。西の悪い魔女はようやく去って行くが、それで一件落着とはいかないようだ。グリンダはドロシーに…

4. What does Glinda advise Dorothy to do?
   (A) Get rid of the Wicked Witch
   (B) Leave Oz immediately
   (C) Sleep safe and sound
   (D) Help the Wizard of Oz

5. Why is Dorothy unable to go home?
   (A) She has nothing to give to the Wizard of Oz.
   (B) She has nobody to go with.
   (C) She does not know her way back.
   (D) She has a bad enemy in Kansas.

6. According to what Glinda says, what is NOT true about the Wizard of Oz?
   (A) He is a good wizard.
   (B) He lives in a city very far away.
   (C) He has already left the Emerald City.
   (D) He is the one who could help Dorothy.

Part 4 グリンダの話を聞き、設問に答えなさい。　38　25

> Part 2 の 3 に続く場面。危険がいまだ去っていないと判断したグリンダは、ド
> ロシーにどのような助言をするだろうか。

7. What will the Munchkins do for Dorothy?
   (A) Welcome her to Munchkinland
   (B) Take her to Munchkinland
   (C) Help her cross the border
   (D) Accompany her to the border

8. What does Glinda tell Dorothy to do?
   (A) Always wear the slippers
   (B) Keep the slippers in a safe
   (C) Put the slippers on when crossing the border
   (D) Take off the slippers at the border

9. What is Dorothy likely to do?
   (A) Beg for the Wicked Witch's mercy
   (B) Go west of Emerald City
   (C) Walk along the brick-paved road
   (D) Find a palace built of bricks

音声を聞き、適切な語句を空所に書き入れなさい。

Part 1

T 34　**S** 21

1. (A) The woman on the (^{1}　　　　　) is (^{2}　　　　　　) at the girl.

　　(B) The woman on the (^{3}　　　　　　) is holding a (^{4}　　　　　　).

　　(C) The girl in the (^{5}　　　　　) is holding a (^{6}　　　　　) (^{7}　　　　　　).

　　(D) All of them are looking in the (^{8}　　　　　) (^{9}　　　　　　).

Part 2

T 35-36　**S** 22-23

2. Who (^{1}　　　　　) my sister? Was it you?

　　(A) No. It was (^{2}　　　　) (^{3}　　　　　　).

　　(B) She is (^{4}　　　　　　), (^{5}　　　　　　) and (^{6}　　　　　) dead.

　　(C) The (^{7}　　　　　) Old Witch at last is dead.

3. Did you bring your (^{8}　　　　　　) with you?

　　(A) Bring me her (^{9}　　　　　　).

　　(B) Yes, it is, (^{10}　　　) (^{11}　　　　　).

　　(C) No, (^{12}　　　) (^{13}　　　　　) I didn't.

Part 3

Glinda: Pooh, what a (¹   ) (²   ) (³   )! I'm afraid

you've made rather a bad (⁴   ) of the Wicked Witch of

the West. The (⁵   ) you get out of Oz altogether, the

(⁶   ) you'll sleep, my dear.

Dorothy: Oh, I'd give anything to get out of Oz altogether, but, which is the

way back to Kansas? I can't go the way I came.

Glinda: No, that's true. The only person who might know would be the

(⁷   ) (⁸   ) (⁹   ) Wizard of Oz himself.

Dorothy: The Wizard of Oz? Is he good or is he wicked?

Glinda: Oh, very good, but very (¹⁰   ). He lives in the

Emerald City and that's a long (¹¹   ) from here.

Part 4

You'll have to (¹   ) to the Emerald City. The Munchkins will see you

(²   ) to the (³   ) of Munchkinland. And remember, never let

those ruby (⁴   ) off your feet (⁵   ) (⁶   ) (⁷   ), or

you will be at the (⁸   ) of the Wicked Witch of the West. (⁹   ),

all you do is follow the Yellow Brick Road. Just follow the Yellow Brick Road.

10. Let the joyous news be spread; the Wicked
Old Witch at _____ is dead!
(A) best
(B) last
(C) least
(D) most

11. We have got to _____ it legally to see if
she is dead.
(A) purify
(B) satisfy
(C) verify
(D) notify

12. This is a day of _____ for all the
Munchkins and their descendants.
(A) independence
(B) independent
(C) independently
(D) independents

13. In the _____ of the Lullaby League, we
wish to welcome you to Munchkinland.
(A) case
(B) face
(C) light
(D) name

14. I did not _____ to kill anybody.
(A) matter
(B) mean
(C) signify
(D) suggest

 Part 2 の 2 に続く場面。東の悪い魔女が履いていたルビーの靴は、いつのまにかドロシーの持ち物になってしまっている。西の悪い魔女は…

Give me back my slippers! I'm the only one that knows ---15--- to use

them. They're ---16--- no use to you. Give them back to me. Give them

back! You stay out of this, Glinda, or I'll fix you as well!

And as ---17--- you, my fine lady, it's true I can't ---18--- you here and

now as I'd like. But just try to stay out of my way. I'll get you, my pretty.

And your little dog, too!

15. (A) as
    (B) how
    (C) what
    (D) which

16. (A) for
    (B) in
    (C) of
    (D) to

17. (A) for
    (B) if
    (C) is
    (D) of

18. (A) abide by
    (B) apply for
    (C) ask for
    (D) attend to

ドロシーたちは竜巻に巻き込まれてカンザスからオズの国まで飛ばされてしまうが、映画撮影当時のカンザスの気候はどうだったのだろうか。

The Wizard of Oz and the American Dust Bowl

When you think of the film *The Wizard of Oz*, dust is perhaps not the first thing that comes to mind. Yet a region called the "Dust Bowl" played an important role in how the story was brought to the big screen.

In the 1930s, a drought hit the central United States. The land had been over-farmed for many years, so the dry soil became loose, and the wind blew it away like dust. Farmers experienced "black storms," or massive clouds of dust blowing across the prairies. Crops failed year after year, and many farmers lost their land as banks foreclosed on mortgages. The worst-hit area was called the "Dust Bowl" and included parts of Kansas.

The Wizard of Oz reflects this state of affairs. In the 1939 film, Aunt Em and Uncle Henry work desperately to keep their farm. When Dorothy's dog Toto bites the spiteful Miss Gulch, she threatens to sue Dorothy's family and take their farm away. Meanwhile, Dorothy dreams of escaping "over the rainbow." She gets her wish when she is caught up in a cyclone as dark and powerful as any black storm. Through these characters and events, the filmmakers contrast the fantasy of Oz with the grim reality of the Dust Bowl years.

Famously, scenes in Kansas are shown in a dusty sepia tone, while Oz pops off the screen in brilliant Technicolor. Technicolor was new and exciting to audiences in 1939, and it displayed a gorgeous world of yellow brick roads, ruby slippers, and the Emerald City. When Dorothy opens the door of her dull, colorless farmhouse onto the radiant Land of Oz, she is leaving the Dust Bowl and its hardships behind. The contrast between the sepia tone and Technicolor must have helped viewers feel a strong affinity with Dorothy and her dreams.

Notes:

fail「不作となる」foreclose on「抵当流れにする」spiteful「意地の悪い」Technicolor「テクニカラー（カラー撮影技術の名前）」radiant「きらびやかな」

19. According to the passage, what is the "Dust Bowl"?
    (A) Dry powder that consists of very small bits of earth
    (B) The distributor of *The Wizard of Oz*
    (C) A region of the United States in the 1930s
    (D) A wide round dish used for holding liquids or food

20. What was the cause of the black storms blowing across the prairies?
    (A) Dryness caused by overfarming
    (B) Global warming
    (C) The greenhouse effect
    (D) Flooding

21. How can the Dust Bowl years be characterized?
    (A) Glorious
    (B) Colorful
    (C) Tough
    (D) Average

22. What is used to represent Dorothy and her family's hard life in Kansas?
    (A) A rainbow
    (B) A sepia tone
    (C) New technology
    (D) Miss Gulch

23. What is true about Technicolor?
    (A) It was still uncommon when the film was released.
    (B) It showed roads, farmhouses, and the whole city in brilliant color.
    (C) It was used only partly in the film due to budget limitations.
    (D) It used film that recorded scenes in seven colors.

時制

---

1. The Wicked Old Witch at last **is** dead.　　　　（現在形）
2. I thoroughly **examined** her.　　　　　　　　　（過去形）
3. You **are going to see** a wizard?　　　　　　　（未来形）
4. You **are traveling** in disguise.　　　　　　　（進行形）
5. She **has gone** where the goblins go.　　　　　（完了形）

　動詞は、それが表す動作や状態がいつのことかによって、さまざまな形式があります。基本的な 5 つの形式とそれぞれの機能を下の表で確認しましょう。

時制の形式と機能

種類	形式と機能
現在形	原形（辞書の見出し語の形）が使われる。主語が三人称単数のときは、-s が付く（例：Mary lives in Tokyo.）。現在の性質や状態、習慣、反復的な出来事を表す。
過去形	-ed が付く。不規則活用をする動詞もある（例：made, took, slept）。すでに起こった出来事や動作、状態を表す。
未来形	前に助動詞 will や am/are/is going to が置かれる。これから起こる出来事や動作、状態を表す。
進行形	現在進行形は［am/are/is+ 現在分詞（-ing 形）］、過去進行形は［was/were+ 現在分詞］、未来進行形は［will be+ 現在分詞］で表される。過去、現在、未来など、ある時点で進行中の動作を表す。
完了形	現在完了形は［have/has+ 過去分詞（-en 形）］、過去完了形は［had+ 過去分詞］、未来完了形は［will have+ 過去分詞］で表される。ある時を基準として、それまでに完了したこと、それまでの経験、それまで継続していることを表す。

Exercises

(　　　) 内から適切な語句を選びましょう。

1. He (listens / is listening) to music when he drives.

2. She sometimes had to check if the computer program (ran / was running) properly.

3. In ancient times, people believed the earth (is / was) flat.

4. I'll send you a text message when I (arrive / will arrive) at the station.

5. I don't know if he (comes / will come) to the party tomorrow.

6. By the time she retires, she (has / will have) worked for this company for 50 years.

ACT 5 If I Had a Brain

 0:32:42-0:40:27

Words & Phrases

次の英単語・フレーズの意味を、下記の語群より選びなさい。　🔵 42

1. bend	( )	6. manage	( )	11. stroll	( )
2. coworker	( )	7. plenty of . . .	( )	12. tedious	( )
3. dozens of . . .	( )	8. raise	( )	13. turn down	( )
4. except	( )	9. slip off	( )	14. ultimate	( )
5. feed	( )	10. magnificent	( )	15. vote	( )

a. 〜を上げる　　d. 究極の　　g. するっと外れる　j. 投票する　　m.（食べ物を）与える
b. うまく取り扱う　e. 断る　　　h. たくさんの〜　　k. ぶらつく　　n. 何ダースもの〜
c. 退屈な　　　　f. 同僚　　　i. 壮大な　　　　l. 〜を除いて　o. 曲げる

Listening Tips

同化（1）

　映画『オズの魔法使』と言えば、劇中歌 *Over the Rainbow*「虹の彼方に」が直ちに連想されます。さて、rainbow（虹）の発音は辞書では /réɪnbòʊ/ と書かれていますが、主人公ジュディー・ガーランドがこの歌を歌っているシーンをよく観察すると、rain- の最後の子音には、/n/ ではなく /m/ という発音を用いていることが分かります。これは、-bow のはじめの子音が /b/ という両方の唇を閉じて発音する「両唇音」であるために、その影響を受けて、rain- の最後の /n/ が両唇音の /m/ に変化したためです。このように、隣接する音の影響を受け、ある音が別の音に変わることを同化 (assimilation) と呼びます。rainbow の場合は、右側の b が左側の n に対して影響を与えているので、このような同化を特に逆行同化 (regressive assimilation) と呼びます。good boy /gʊd bɔɪ/ が /gʊb bɔɪ/ になったり、good girl /gʊd gə:rl/ が /gʊg gə:rl/ になったりするのも逆行同化の例です。

Exercises ━━━━━━━━━━━━━━━━ 🔵 43 Ⓢ 26 ━

次の台詞の（　　　　　）内を聞き取り、同化に注意して全文を音読しましょう。

1. (　　　　　)(　　　　　). That way is a very nice way.

2. (　　　　　)(　　　　　) silly, Toto. Scarecrows don't talk.

3. Are you doing that (　　　) (　　　　　　), or can't you make up your mind?

Part 1 写真の場面を最も適切に表している音声を選びなさい。　🎧 44　Ⓢ 27

1. Ⓐ Ⓑ Ⓒ Ⓓ

Part 2 問いかけに対する最も適切な応答を選びなさい。　🎧45-46　Ⓢ 28-29

Part 3 に続く場面。黄色いレンガ道でのドロシーとかかしの会話である。ドロシーの話に出てくる地名をかかしは知らないようで…

2. Ⓐ Ⓑ Ⓒ

ドロシーはかかしに、故郷に帰してくれと頼むために魔法使いに会いに行く途中だと話す。それを聞いたかかしはドロシーに…

3. Ⓐ Ⓑ Ⓒ

Part 3 会話を聞き、設問に答えなさい。　🎧 47　Ⓢ 30
（登場話者：Dorothy, Scarecrow）

マンチキンたちの国を出たドロシーは、十字路に出てしまう。どちらの道を行こうか迷っていると、かかしが話しかけてくる。

4. What is true about Dorothy and Scarecrow?
　(A) They have been standing there all day long.
　(B) They are meeting for the first time.
　(C) They hate each other.
　(D) They are close friends.

5. How does Scarecrow feel about having to stand upright all day?
   (A) Horrified
   (B) Comfortable
   (C) Bored
   (D) Fulfilled

6. What will Dorothy most likely do next?
   (A) Give Scarecrow a hand
   (B) Turn down Scarecrow's request
   (C) Stop talking with Scarecrow
   (D) Fall down on her knees

Part 4 かかしの話を聞き、設問に答えなさい。

 脳みそをもらうために、自分も連れて行って欲しいと頼むかかしだが、ドロシーは悪い魔女に邪魔されるかもしれないと言う。かかしは…

7. What is Scarecrow afraid of?
   (A) Witches
   (B) Light
   (C) Fire
   (D) Nothing

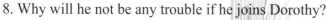

8. Why will he not be any trouble if he joins Dorothy?
   (A) There is plenty of food.
   (B) He can feed Dorothy.
   (C) He can eat by himself.
   (D) He does not eat anything.

9. What will he not try to do because he cannot think?
   (A) Take a chance
   (B) Save his face
   (C) Take control
   (D) Look after Dorothy

Dictation

音声を聞き、適切な語句を空所に書き入れなさい。

Part 1

T 44   **S** 27

1. (A) Many flowers are (^{1}) around the scarecrow.

   (B) A (^{2}) is (^{3}) over the scarecrow's head.

   (C) The scarecrow is (^{4}) his left hand.

   (D) The scarecrow is looking at his right hand.

Part 2

T 45-46   **S** 28-29

2. Where's Kansas?

   (A) I could (^{1}) (^{2}) the hours.

   (B) That's (^{3}) I live.

   (C) We've been walking (^{4}) (^{5}) (^{6}).

3. Won't you take me (^{7}) you?

   (A) I won't be (^{8}) (^{9}).

   (B) Yes, that's (^{10}).

   (C) (^{11}), of course I will.

Part 3

Dorothy: How do you do?

Scarecrow: How do you do?

Dorothy: Very well, thank you.

Scarecrow: Oh, I'm not feeling at all well. You see, it's very (^{1}) being

(^{2}) (^{3}) here all day long with a pole up your back.

Dorothy: Oh dear, that must be terribly uncomfortable. Can't you get down?

Scarecrow: Down? No, you see, I'm . . . well, I'm . . .

Dorothy: Oh, well. Here, (^{4}) (^{5}) help you.

Scarecrow: Oh, that's very (^{6}) (^{7}) (^{8}), very kind.

Dorothy: Well . . . oh, dear. I don't (^{9}) (^{10}) how I can . . .

Scarecrow: Of course, I'm not bright about doing things . . . but if you'll just bend

the nail down in back, maybe I'll (^{11}) (^{12}) and . . .

Dorothy: Oh yes.

Part 4

Witch? Huh! I'm not afraid of a witch! I'm not afraid of anything. (^{1})

a (^{2}) (^{3}). But I'd (^{4}) a whole box (^{5})

(^{6}) them for the (^{7}) of getting some brains. Look. I won't be

any trouble, because I don't eat a thing, and I won't try to (^{8}) things,

because I can't think. Won't you take me with you?

10. Are you doing that _____ purpose, or
 can't you make up your mind?
 (A) on
 (B) in
 (C) of
 (D) with

11. I just thought you hurt _____.
 (A) you
 (B) yours
 (C) yourself
 (D) to you

12. With the thoughts you will be thinking, you
 could be _____ Lincoln.
 (A) the
 (B) same
 (C) other
 (D) another

13. Even if the Wizard did not give you any
 brains, you would be _____ off than you
 are now.
 (A) more worse
 (B) no bad
 (C) no worse
 (D) none the less

14. I will show you _____ apples.
 (A) get
 (B) to get
 (C) what to get
 (D) how to get

 ドロシー出発の場面。マンチキンの見送りの歌（♪「黄色いレンガの道をたどって」）と原作の描写を合わせて鑑賞してみよう。

She bade her friends good-bye, and again started along the road of yellow brick.

> ---15--- the Yellow Brick Road
> You are ---16--- to see the Wizard
> The Wonderful Wizard of Oz
> You will find he is a whiz of a Wiz'
>
> If ever, oh, ever a Wiz' there was
> The Wizard of Oz is one
> ---17--- of the wonderful things he does

When she had gone several miles she thought she would stop ---18---.

15. (A) Follow
　　(B) Follow to
　　(C) Follow-up
　　(D) Follower

16. (A) off
　　(B) on
　　(C) at
　　(D) in

17. (A) As
　　(B) Ahead
　　(C) A bit
　　(D) Because

18. (A) rest
　　(B) resting
　　(C) to rest
　　(D) rested

本作で主要キャラクターのひとりとして登場する「かかし」だが、アメリカでは
かかしフェスティバルなるものがあるようだ。

Sensational Scarecrow Display in Dorothy Gardens

Come to Dorothy Gardens this October for the Scarecrow Festival!
Stroll through our magnificent gardens in all their seasonal glory, and
marvel at dozens of eye-popping scarecrows made by the community.
Enjoy tasty treats, carnival rides, local musicians, and craft kiosks. It's the
ultimate family outing. Festival admission FREE for garden visitors!

Scarecrow Festival
10 am – 6 pm each day

**Festival Fair : Saturdays
and Sundays only**
Food, crafts, rides, games,
and live performances at the
Pumpkin Patch Outdoor Theater

Make Your Own Scarecrow
Make the scarecrow of your
dreams come alive! Team
up with family, friends, and
coworkers, and compete for
fantastic prizes.

PRIZES

ALL ENTRIES
　—4 tickets to Dorothy Gardens
GRAND PRIZE ($600 VALUE!)
　*Visitors vote for their favorite
　scarecrow and the winner will be
　announced on the last day.
　—Trophy
　—$300 The Mall Gift Card
　—Dinner for 4 at Harvest
Restaurant ($100 value)
　—1 night stay at the Garden Hotel
($200 value)
JUDGES' PICK
　—Trophy
　—$200 The Mall Gift Card
　—Dinner for 4 at Harvest
Restaurant ($100 value)

19. What does the Scarecrow Festival NOT feature?
    (A) Delicious dishes
    (B) Amusement rides
    (C) A gardening competition
    (D) Musical performances

20. In the advertisement, the word "eye-popping" in paragraph 1, line 3 is closest in meaning to
    (A) impressive
    (B) luxurious
    (C) prize-winning
    (D) visible

21. When will the Scarecrow Festival be held?
    (A) All year round
    (B) Only on weekends
    (C) Throughout the holiday season
    (D) In autumn

22. What can festival visitors do on weekdays?
    (A) Nothing
    (B) Make scarecrows
    (C) Carve pumpkins
    (D) Attend an award ceremony

23. What is true about the prizes?
    (A) The winner of the Grand Prize is chosen by judges.
    (B) Not all entries will get a prize.
    (C) Only the winner of the Grand Prize is awarded a trophy.
    (D) The Judges' Pick is worth half as much as the Grand Prize.

名詞

---

1. **Scarecrows** don't talk. （普通名詞）
2. It's a man made out of **tin**! （物質名詞）
3. **People** do go both ways. （集合名詞）
4. She brings you good **news**. （抽象名詞）
5. Where's **Kansas**? （固有名詞）

名詞は事物の名を表し、普通名詞、物質名詞、集合名詞、抽象名詞、固有名詞の 5 種類があります。

名詞の種類と機能

種　類	機　　能
普通名詞	目に見えて、一定の輪郭を持つものを表す。単数のときは a や the（冠詞）などをつけ、複数のときは通常 -s を語尾に付ける（複数形）。例：book, student
物質名詞	液体や気体など、一定の輪郭を持たない物質の名を表す。複数形にはならない。例：coffee, light, chocolate, wine, gasoline, money, sound, water
集合名詞	集合体の名を表す。単数扱いのときと複数扱いのときがある。例：police, family, class, government, team, public, people, furniture
抽象名詞	性質、状態、思考など、抽象的な概念を表す。複数形にはならない。例：knowledge, peace, advice, music, information, experience, marriage
固有名詞	人物、場所、国などの名前を表し、原則として複数形にはならない。例：Einstein, Morocco, the Thames, the Alps, the Eiffel Tower, Venus

Exercises

(　　　) 内から適切な語句を選びましょう。

1. She has (a smart / smart) boyfriend.

2. I ordered (two / two cups of) coffee: one for my friend, the other for myself.

3. They are a family who often (quarrel among themselves / quarrels among itself).

4. I would appreciate it if you could give me some (advice / advices) about my presentation.

5. He is going to be (Edison / an Edison) in the future.

Aᴄᴛ 6 If I Had a Heart

 0:40:27-0:47:55

Words & Phrases

次の英単語・フレーズの意味を、下記の語群より選びなさい。　🔵52

1. axe	( )	6. fix	( )	11. polish	( )
2. chop	( )	7. hollow	( )	12. rust	( )
3. cruel	( )	8. lack	( )	13. sew	( )
4. decade	( )	9. lazy	( )	14. fasten	( )
5. destination	( )	10. peel	( )	15. stuff	( )

a. くくりつける　　d. 10年間　　　g. 修理する　　j. 磨く　　m. たたき切る（こと）
b. （皮を）むく　　e. さびる　　　h. 怠惰な　　　k. 斧　　　n. 不足している
c. 空の、空洞の　　f. 残酷な　　　i. 目的地　　　l. 縫う　　o. 詰め物をする

Listening Tips

同化（2）

　Act 5 では、逆行同化について学びました。同化にはこの他にも、前の音が後ろの音に影響を及ぼす進行同化 (progressive assimilation) があります。bacon [béɪkən → béɪkn → béɪkŋ] や happen [hǽpən → hǽpn → hǽpm] は進行同化の例です（ここでは、まず、/ə/ の脱落 (elision) が起こってから同化が起こっています）。さらに、miss you [mís ju → míʃu]、need you [níːd ju → níːdʒu]、want you [wánt ju → wántʃu] などは相互同化 (reciprocal assimilation) と呼ばれます。一般的に、ゆっくりと注意深く話す場合より、早口で形式張らずに話す方が同化は起こりやすいものの、同化は必ず起こらなければならないというものではありません。とは言え、同化が起こったときにどのような発音になるかを知っておくことは、リスニング力の向上には必要です。

Exercises ──────────── 🔵53 Ⓢ32

次の台詞の（　　　）内を聞き取り、同化に注意して全文を音読しましょう。

1. (　　　) (　　　) say something?

2. Where do you (　　　) (　　　) be oiled first?

3. About a year ago, I was chopping that tree when suddenly it (　　　) (　　　) rain.

Part 1 写真の場面を最も適切に表している音声を選びなさい。 54 Ⓢ 33

1. Ⓐ Ⓑ Ⓒ Ⓓ

Part 2 問いかけに対する最も適切な応答を選びなさい。 Ⓣ 55-56 Ⓢ 34-35

 旅を続けるドロシーとかかしは、その途中でブリキでできた木こりに出会う。油差しをとってくれという木こりに、ドロシーは…

2. Ⓐ Ⓑ Ⓒ

 Part 4 に続く場面。ドロシーがブリキの木こりを励ますために口にした言葉に反応して、別の人物が割り込んで話しかけてくる。

3. Ⓐ Ⓑ Ⓒ

Part 3 会話を聞き、設問に答えなさい。 Ⓣ 57 Ⓢ 36

（登場話者：Tin Man, Dorothy, Scarecrow）

 Part 2 の 2 の少し後の場面。ブリキ男が自分の身の上話や、これまでのいきさつを話している。彼には悩みがあるようで…

4. How long had Tin Man been holding up his axe?
   (A) About a year
   (B) Many years
   (C) A few decades
   (D) One generation

5. Why does Scarecrow say, "Beautiful!"
   (A) He thinks that Tin Man is good-looking.
   (B) He thinks it is a fine day.
   (C) He sees Tin Man moving smoothly.
   (D) He hears a good banging sound.

6. What did the tin-smith forget to do?
   (A) Give Tin Man a heart
   (B) Oil Tin Man's mouth
   (C) Coat Tin Man with silver
   (D) Fix Tin Man's chest

Part 4 ドロシーの話を聞き、設問に答えなさい。　 58　 37

Part 3 の後の場面。ブリキ男の悩みを聞いたドロシーは、彼にどんなことを言っているのだろうか。ドロシーの提案を聞いてみよう。

7. What did Dorothy think about how Tin Man moved?
   (A) It was excellent.
   (B) It had some problems but was good overall.
   (C) It was poor but had a few good points.
   (D) It was terrible and had no merit at all.

8. What does she suggest to Tin Man?
   (A) He should improve his performance.
   (B) He should wander in the heart of the city.
   (C) He should go with them to their destination.
   (D) He should bring the Wizard to the Emerald City.

9. What does she expect the Wizard to do?
   (A) Hurt Tin Man's heart
   (B) Provide Tin Man with what he lacks
   (C) Change Tin Man's mind
   (D) Take Tin Man to the Emerald City

音声を聞き、適切な語句を空所に書き入れなさい。

Part 1

T 54 **S** 33

1. (A) The girl is (^{1}) (^{2}) an apple.

   (B) The girl is (^{3}) an apple.

   (C) The girl is (^{4}) an apple.

   (D) The girl is (^{5}) an apple.

Part 2

T 55-56 **S** 34-35

2. Where do you want to be (^{1}) (^{2})?

   (A) Oil (^{3})! Oil (^{4})!

   (B) My mouth, my mouth!

   (C) Yes. Oh, look!

3. We've come such a long way already.

   (A) You call that long? Why, you've (^{5}) (^{6}).

   (B) You weren't around when I was (^{7}) and (^{8}) together.

   (C) I was standing over there (^{9}) for the (^{10}) (^{11}).

Part 3

Tin Man:　I've held that (^{1}　　　) up (^{2}　　　) (^{3}　　　).

Dorothy:　Oh, (^{4}　　　)! How did you (^{5}　　　) get like this?

Tin Man:　Oh, well, about a year ago, I was (^{6}　　　) that tree when suddenly it began to rain. And (^{7}　　　) in the middle of a chop, I rusted (^{8}　　　). And I've been that way ever since.

Dorothy:　Well, you're perfect now.

Tin Man:　Perfect? Oh, (^{9}　　　) (^{10}　　　) my (^{11}　　　) if you think I'm perfect. Go ahead, (^{12}　　　) (^{13}　　　) it!

Scarecrow:　Beautiful! What (^{14}　　　) (^{15}　　　)!

Tin Man:　It's empty. The (^{16}　　　) forgot to give me a heart.

Dorothy & Scarecrow:　No heart!?

Tin Man:　No heart! All (^{17}　　　).

Part 4

You're a little (^{1}　　　) yet, but your movement was wonderful! You know, we were just (^{2}　　　) why you couldn't come with us to the Emerald City to ask the Wizard of Oz (^{3}　　　) (^{4}　　　) (^{5}　　　). He must give you one when we get there. We've come such a long way already.

10. _____ the Wizard would not give me a
    heart when we got there?
    (A) Consider
    (B) Regard
    (C) Suppose
    (D) Presume

11. I will see you reach the Wizard, _____
    I get a heart or not.
    (A) how
    (B) why
    (C) which
    (D) whether

12. Let her _____ and make a beehive out of
    me!
    (A) try
    (B) to try
    (C) trying
    (D) tried

13. I feel as if I _____ you all the time.
    (A) will know
    (B) am knowing
    (C) am known
    (D) had known

14. Still, I wish I _____ when I met you.
    (A) remember
    (B) am remembering
    (C) am remembered
    (D) could remember

ドロシーとかかしがブリキ男に出会う場面は、原作ではどのように描写されているだろうか。

One of ---15--- had been partly chopped through, and standing beside it, with an uplifted axe in his hands, ---16--- a man made entirely of tin. His head and arms and legs were jointed upon his body, but he stood perfectly ---17---, as if ---18---.

15. (A) a big tree
    (B) big trees
    (C) the big tree
    (D) the big trees

16. (A) was
    (B) were
    (C) have been
    (D) will be

17. (A) motion
    (B) motionless
    (C) moved
    (D) movement

18. (A) he had been groaning for a year
    (B) he were well oiled
    (C) he could not stir at all
    (D) it were about to rain

ブリキの木こりは、なぜブリキの体になったのだろうか。木こりの語る身の上話を原作の英文で味わってみよう。

There was one of the Munchkin girls who was so beautiful that I soon grew to love her with all my heart. She, on her part, promised to marry me as soon as I could earn enough money to build a better house for her; so I set to work harder than ever. —[1]—. But the girl lived with an old woman who did not want her to marry anyone, for she was so lazy she wished the girl to remain with her and do the cooking and the housework. So the old woman went to the wicked Witch of the East, and promised her two sheep and a cow if she would prevent the marriage. Thereupon the wicked Witch enchanted my axe, and when I was chopping away at my best one day, for I was anxious to get the new house and my wife as soon as possible, the axe slipped all at once and cut off my left leg. —[2]—.

This at first seemed a great misfortune, for I knew a one-legged man could not do very well as a wood-chopper. So I went to a tin-smith and had him make me a new leg out of tin. The leg worked very well, once I was used to it; but my action angered the wicked Witch of the East, for she had promised the old woman I should not marry the pretty Munchkin girl. When I began chopping again my axe slipped and cut off my right leg. Again I went to the tinner, and again he made me a leg out of tin. After this the enchanted axe cut off my arms, one after the other; but, nothing daunted, I had them replaced with tin ones. The wicked Witch then made the axe slip and cut off my head, and at first I thought that was the end of me. But the tinner happened to come along, and he made me a new head out of tin. —[3]—.

I thought I had beaten the wicked Witch then, and I worked harder than ever; but I little knew how cruel my enemy could be. She thought of a new way to kill my love for the beautiful Munchkin maiden, and made my axe slip again, so that it cut right through my body, splitting me into two halves. Once more the tinner came to my help and made me a body of tin, fastening my tin arms and legs and head to it, by means of joints, so that I could move around as well as ever. But, alas! I had now no heart, so that I lost all my love for the Munchkin girl, and did not care whether I married her or not. —[4]—.

19. What was the man told to do to marry the beautiful girl?
    (A) Build a better house for them to live in
    (B) Make money to buy a comfortable house
    (C) Repair the girl's house as soon as possible
    (D) Live with the old woman as well as the girl

20. Why did the old woman not want the girl to marry anyone?
    (A) She loved the girl with all her heart.
    (B) The Witch insisted that the girl should not marry anyone.
    (C) The Witch wanted all women to be independent from men.
    (D) She wanted the girl to do all the housework for her.

21. What did the Witch of the East do to the man to prevent the marriage?
    (A) She enchanted his arms and legs so that he could not move.
    (B) She cast a spell on his axe to make it slip.
    (C) She fastened his arms and limbs to a tree.
    (D) She took his heart out of his body with her own hands.

22. Why has the man become indifferent to his marriage with the girl?
    (A) He no longer has a heart.
    (B) He fell in love with another girl.
    (C) He looks different than before.
    (D) He is under the influence of magic.

23. In which of the positions marked [1], [2], [3] and [4] does the following sentence best belong?
    "I suppose she is still living with the old woman, waiting for me to come after her."
    (A) [1]
    (B) [2]
    (C) [3]
    (D) [4]

形容詞・副詞

---

1. You're off to see the **wonderful** wizard of Oz.　（形容詞・限定用法）
2. You're **perfect** now.　（形容詞・叙述用法）
3. Now, I'm **awfully** sorry.　（副詞・程度）
4. **Luckily**, the tin-smith made me some ears.　（副詞・文修飾）
5. Professor Marvel **never** guesses.　（副詞・頻度）

　形容詞や副詞は、文の内容を正しく理解する上で重要です。品詞については Act 1 と Act 2 で学習しましたが、形容詞と副詞の用法をここでもう一度確認しましょう。

　形容詞は、名詞や代名詞を修飾したり、補語になったりします。形容詞には、名詞の前や後ろに置かれてその名詞の性質や状態を説明する＜限定用法＞と、補語の位置に置かれて主語や目的語についての説明を加える＜叙述用法＞があります。

She picked a beautiful flower.　＜限定用法＞
This movie is very exciting.　　＜叙述用法＞

これらの例では、形容詞 beautiful が名詞 flower の前に置かれ、「美しい花」であると名詞 flower を説明しており、また、形容詞 exciting が動詞 is の補語として使われ、主語 this movie について「この映画はわくわくする」と説明を加えています。

　副詞は、動詞・形容詞・他の副詞または文全体を修飾します。形容詞・副詞を修飾するときは、副詞はその前に置かれますが、動詞を修飾するときは副詞の持つ意味や文脈により位置はさまざまです。文を修飾する場合、文頭や文末に置かれることもあります。ただし、頻度を表す副詞（often, always など）は助動詞・be 動詞のあと、一般動詞の前に置かれます。

Exercises

（　　　）内から適切な語句を選びましょう。

1. "Hi, haven't I seen you somewhere before?" "No, I'm (sure / surely) that you haven't."

2. My brother was particularly (friend / friendly) with her.

3. It is (wide / widely) known that rapid industrialization is one of the causes of environmental pollution in this country.

4. There is (scarce / scarcely) any place left in this town where you can get close to nature.

5. (Hardly / Immediately) had the Prime Minister started to speak when someone in the audience interrupted her.

Aᴄᴛ 7 If I Had the Nerve

 0:47:55-0:58:21

Words & Phrases

次の英単語・フレーズの意味を、下記の語群より選びなさい。 **T2** 02

1. bring about （　） 6. fortunate （　） 11. intimidate （　）
2. courage （　） 7. get along with . . . （　） 12. rush （　）
3. coward （　） 8. heedless （　） 13. shiver （　）
4. disease （　） 9. intelligent （　） 14. sneak up （　）
5. encounter （　） 10. put up with . . . （　） 15. straw （　）

a. 急いで行く　　d. 運のよい　　g. 臆病者　　j. 震える　　m. 注意を払わない
b. 偶然出会う　　e. 脅迫する　　h. 知的な　　k. 麦わら　　n. 〜を我慢する
c. 引き起こす　　f. 忍び寄る　　i. 病気　　　l. 勇気　　　o. 〜と仲良くやっていく

Listening Tips

母音の聞き取り（1）

　Act 7 から 10 の Listening Tips では、標準的なアメリカ英語の発音をもとに、多くの日本人英語学習者が特に聞き分けを不得手としている英語の音を取り上げます。Act 7 と 8 で扱うのは「母音」です。母音は、口が開いた状態で、有声音の呼気が舌や唇などによって阻害されず、比較的自由に流れていく場合に産出されます。母音の音質は、舌の最高点の位置［高い／低い］および［前／後ろ］と唇の形［平唇／円唇］によって決まります。例えば、seat の母音 /iː/ は［高い／前／平唇］ですし、food の母音 /uː/ は［高い／後ろ／円唇］です。

　Exercises の /iː/ や /uː/ は、それぞれ、/ɪ/ や /ʊ/ を単に「伸ばしたもの」ではなく、そもそも、音質が違うことに注意が必要です。たとえば、/iː/ は /ɪ/ に比べてはるかに強く、唇が強く横に引かれ緊張母音 (tense vowel) と呼ばれることがあります。これに対して、/ɪ/ は弛緩母音 (lax vowel) と呼ばれます。なお、弛緩母音 /ɪ/ と /ʊ/ は、それぞれ、/i/ と /u/ で表記されることもあります。

Exercises ──────────────────────── **T2** 03 Ⓢ 38

音声を聞いて、発音されているものに○をつけましょう。

1. /iː/ /ɪ/　　a. seat sit　　b. seat sit　　c. feel fill　　d. feel fill
2. /uː/ /ʊ/　　a. food foot　　b. food foot　　c. pool pull　　d. pool pull

Part 1 写真の場面を最も適切に表している音声を選びなさい。　04 Ⓢ 39

1. Ⓐ Ⓑ Ⓒ Ⓓ

Part 2 問いかけに対する最も適切な応答を選びなさい。　🅣₂05-06 Ⓢ 40-41

 Part 4 に続く場面。ライオンは強そうに見えるが実は怖がりで、夜も眠れないのだという。ブリキ男はライオンに…

2. Ⓐ Ⓑ Ⓒ

 2 に続く場面。勇気がなくて大変困っているというライオンの話を聞いて、ブリキ男はドロシーにひとつの提案をする。

3. Ⓐ Ⓑ Ⓒ

Part 3 会話を聞き、設問に答えなさい。　🅣₂07　Ⓢ 42
　　　　　（登場話者：Dorothy, Scarecrow, Tin Man）

 Part 2 に先行する場面。エメラルドの都を目指して旅をするドロシーたちは、暗い森の中を歩いている。森はいかにも薄気味悪く…

4. Where are they?
　(A) In the middle of the woods
　(B) In the center of a plain
　(C) At the bottom of a valley
　(D) On the edge of a cliff

5. What does Tin Man think will happen?
   (A) It will soon get lighter.
   (B) They will encounter dangerous creatures.
   (C) They will have to eat wild animals.
   (D) They will lose their way.

6. Which animals are NOT mentioned?
   (A) Lions
   (B) Tigers
   (C) Zebras
   (D) Bears

Part 4 ライオンの話を聞き、設問に答えなさい。　　　⓬08　Ⓢ43

Part 3 と Part 2 の間の場面。暗い森を歩くドロシーたちの前に現れたライオンは、三人にどんなことを言っているだろうか。

7. What is Lion trying to do?
   (A) Put up with hunger
   (B) Intimidate the strangers
   (C) Pull an axe out of a tree
   (D) Get along with his friends

8. How is he going to face his enemies?
   (A) Standing on all fours
   (B) With his ears up
   (C) With his paws tied
   (D) With his eyes closed

9. What can be inferred about the listeners?
   (A) They want to make friends with Lion.
   (B) They feel fortunate to see Lion.
   (C) They are frightened of Lion.
   (D) They had long wanted to see Lion.

Dictation

音声を聞き、適切な語句を空所に書き入れなさい。

Part 1

T2 04 S 39

1. (A) The girl is (^{1}) her eyes with her hands.

   (B) The girl is (^{2}) with fallen (^{3}).

   (C) The girl is sleeping (^{4}) by flowers.

   (D) The girl is (^{5}) with her eyes open.

Part 2

T2 05-06 S 40-41

2. Why don't you (^{1}) (^{2}) sheep?

   (A) That doesn't (^{3}) (^{4}) (^{5}). I'm afraid of them.

   (B) I haven't slept (^{6}) (^{7}).

   (C) Because of the wonderful things he does.

3. Don't you think the Wizard (^{8}) (^{9}) him?

   (A) No, it isn't.

   (B) Yeah, it's sad.

   (C) I don't see (^{10}) (^{11}).

Part 3

T2 07 S 42

Dorothy: I don't like this (^{1})! It's dark and (^{2})!

Scarecrow: Of course, I don't know, but I think it'll get (^{3}) before it

gets (^{4}).

Dorothy: Do, do you (^{5}) we'll (^{6}) any wild animals?

Tin Man: Mmmm, we might.

Dorothy: Oh!

Scarecrow: Animals that . . . that (^{7}) (^{8})?

Tin Man: Ah, (^{9}), but (^{10}) lions and tigers and bears.

Dorothy: Lions?

Scarecrow: And tigers?

Tin Man: And bears!

Part 4

T2 08 S 43

Hah! Put your hands up! Put them up! Which one of you first? I'll fight you both

together, if you want. I'll fight you with one (^{1}) (^{2}) behind my

back! I'll fight you standing on one foot! I'll fight you with my eyes closed. Oh,

pulling an axe on me, eh? (^{3}) up on me, eh? Why . . . Oh, scared,

huh? Afraid, huh? How long can you stay fresh in that can? Come on, get up and

fight, you (^{4}) junk yard! Put your hands up, you lopsided bag of

(^{5})!

10. You are _____ a great big coward.
    (A) quite something
    (B) like anything
    (C) all or nothing
    (D) nothing but

11. I do not have _____ courage at all.
    (A) no
    (B) a
    (C) any
    (D) some

12. There is Emerald City! Oh, we are almost there _____.
    (A) at last
    (B) at first
    (C) at a loss
    (D) at most

13. It is no use _____ at a time like this. Nobody will hear you!
    (A) scream
    (B) screaming
    (C) screams
    (D) screamed

14. Look! Emerald City is closer and prettier _____.
    (A) of all
    (B) for a while
    (C) as nothing
    (D) than ever

ドロシーたちが森の中でライオンの「襲撃」を受ける場面は、原作ではどのように描かれているだろうか。原文を読み、映像と比較してみよう。

Little Toto, ---15--- that he had an enemy to face, ran ---16--- toward the

Lion, and the great beast had opened his mouth to bite the dog, when

Dorothy, fearing Toto would be killed, and heedless of danger, rushed

forward and slapped the Lion upon his nose as ---17--- as she could, while

she cried out: "Don't you dare to bite Toto! You ought to be ashamed of

yourself, a big beast like you, ---18--- a poor little dog!"

15. (A) since
    (B) now
    (C) for
    (D) in

16. (A) bark
    (B) to bark
    (C) barked
    (D) barking

17. (A) hard
    (B) hardly
    (C) harder
    (D) hardest

18. (A) bite
    (B) to bite
    (C) bit
    (D) bitten

ドロシーたちがライオンと話をする原作の場面を SNS のグループチャット形式で現代風にアレンジした。

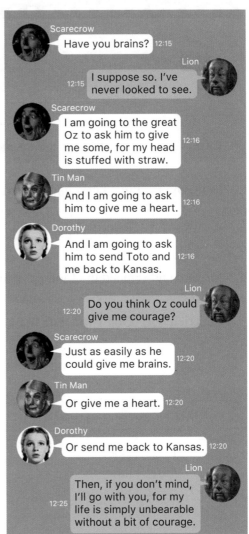

19. What does Dorothy want to know?
    (A) Why Lion lacks bravery
    (B) How Lion became the King of Beasts
    (C) Who Lion really is
    (D) Where Lion is from

20. What does Lion think about his own personality?
    (A) It should remain as it is.
    (B) It does not match his status as King of Beasts.
    (C) It must bring Lion great sorrow.
    (D) It can never be changed.

21. What is Tin Man's opinion about Lion's heart?
    (A) A good doctor could take care of his heart disease.
    (B) Lion should give his heart to Tin Man.
    (C) Lion should appreciate the fact that at least he has a heart.
    (D) A heart makes Lion a coward.

22. At 12:15, what does Scarecrow mean when he writes, "Have you brains?"
    (A) He wants to know if Lion and he both have similar worries.
    (B) He is trying to say that Lion must be an idiot.
    (C) He thinks that Lion should consider the problem seriously.
    (D) He is asking whether Lion has any intelligent friends.

23. What does Lion think about his current situation?
    (A) He cannot stand it any longer.
    (B) He is quite content with it.
    (C) He wants to blame it on somebody else.
    (D) He wonders how it was brought about.

Grammar Training

---

1. You want **to see** other lands. （不定詞・名詞的用法）
2. You've nothing **to be** afraid of. （不定詞・形容詞的用法）
3. *The Wonderful Wizard of Oz* was written **to please** the children of today.
   （不定詞・副詞的用法）
4. Dorothy, stop **imagining** things. （動名詞・動詞の目的語）
5. I never do anything without **consulting** my crystal first.
   （動名詞・前置詞の目的語）

---

1. 名詞的用法（～すること）
   文の主語・目的語・補語として働く。
2. 形容詞的用法（～するための）
   名詞や代名詞を後ろから修飾する。また、自動詞（例：appear, seem など）の補語としても働く。
3. 副詞的用法（～するために、～して、～するとは、など）
   目的・結果・原因 / 理由・判断の根拠・条件などを表し、副詞として働く。

　＜動詞の原形＋ -ing ＞で、「～すること」という意味を持つものを動名詞といいます。動名詞には、文の主語・目的語・補語になるという名詞的性質と、あとに目的語や補語を伴ったり、副詞に修飾されたりするという動詞的性質があります。

※ to 不定詞と動名詞のどちらが後続するかは、その動詞によって決まる。
　　動名詞が後続：mind, enjoy, give up, avoid, finish, escape, put off, stop など
　　to 不定詞が後続：ask, want, aim, agree, expect, decide, fail, manage など
　　両方が後続：attempt, intend, plan, like, start, neglect, begin など
　　どちらが後続するかで意味が変わるもの：remember, forget, try, regret など

Exercises

(　　　) 内から適切な語句を選びましょう。

1. Mary lets her children (have / to have) their own way, so they stay up late every night.

2. Ken never fails (sending / to send) a birthday present to his father.

3. We should avoid (eating / to eat) too much sugar.

4. The nurse told us not (entering / to enter) the room because the patient was undergoing treatment.

5. You will regret (not following / not to follow) my advice.

Aᴄᴛ 8 Knock, and It Shall Be . . .

0:58:21-1:03:56

Words & Phrases

次の英単語・フレーズの意味を、下記の語群より選びなさい。　T2 12

1. a couple of . . .	(　)	6. company	(　)	11. prosperous	(　)
2. audience	(　)	7. fairly	(　)	12. row	(　)
3. bald	(　)	8. follow	(　)	13. state	(　)
4. beard	(　)	9. messy	(　)	14. tidy up	(　)
5. business	(　)	10. mustache	(　)	15. waste	(　)

a. あごひげ　　　d. 2, 3 の〜　　g. 謁見、聴衆　　j. かなり、相当に　　m. 繁栄している
b. 口ひげ　　　　e. 後を追う　　　h. 同行、仲間　　k. 散らかった、汚い　　n. 身ぎれいにする
c. 禿げた　　　　f. 浪費する　　　i. 用事、商売　　l. はっきり述べる　　o. （横の）列

Listening Tips

母音の聞き取り（2）

　Exercises の問題 1 は、後半部分で音の変化がある二重母音 /ou/ なのか、音が一定の /ɔː/ なのかを判断して聞き分けます。2 の barn /bɑːrn/（納屋）の /ɑːr/ は口の開きが大きく舌を低く奥に置くのに対して、burn /bəːrn/（燃える）の /əːr/（記号 /ɝː/ が使われることもある）は口の開きが大きくなく、舌が高くも低くもない位置にあり、舌全体をやや奥に引いて発音します。3 の pat /pæt/（なでる）の /æ/ は口を大きく開くとともに、唇も左右に大きく広げ、舌全体を前寄りの低い位置に置いて発音します。pot /pɑt/（ポット；鍋）の /ɑ/ は口を大きく開き、舌を低い位置に置くとともに、舌を奥に引いて発音します。putt /pʌt/（《ゴルフ》パット）の /ʌ/ は日本語の「ア」ほど口の開きは大きくなく、口の開きも舌の位置も中間の音です。ちなみに、「ピザハット」や「リンガーハット」の「ハット」は hut /hʌt/（小屋）であり、hat /hæt/（帽子）ではありません。

Exercises　T2 13 Ⓢ 44

音声を聞いて、発音されているものに○をつけましょう。

1. /ou/ /ɔː/	a. low law	b. low law	c. hole hall	d. hole hall
2. /ɑːr/ /əːr/	a. barn burn	b. barn burn	c. star stir	d. star stir
3. /æ/ /ɑ/ /ʌ/	a. pat pot putt	b. pat pot putt	c. hat hot hut	d. hat hot hut

Part 1 写真の場面を最も適切に表している音声を選びなさい。 **T2** 14 **S** 45

1. Ⓐ Ⓑ Ⓒ Ⓓ

Part 2 問いかけに対する最も適切な応答を選びなさい。 **T2**15-16 **S** 46-47

エメラルドの都の中に入ったドロシーたち。そこに馬車が現れ、御者はどこでも連れて行ってやるという。ドロシーはそれに答えて…

2. Ⓐ Ⓑ Ⓒ

Part 6 直前の場面。エメラルドの都に突如悪い魔女が現れ、ドロシーを引き渡せというメッセージを飛行機雲で描く。慌てたドロシーは…

3. Ⓐ Ⓑ Ⓒ

Part 3 会話を聞き、設問に答えなさい。 **T2** 17 **S** 48
（登場話者：Doorman, Dorothy, Scarecrow）

ドロシーたちはエメラルドの都にたどりついたが、入り口の門が閉まっていて入れない。すったもんだの末、門番を呼び出すと…

4. Why has Dorothy come?
   (A) To exchange greetings with the doorman
   (B) To start a new business with the Great Oz
   (C) To have a good time in the city
   (D) To request an audience with the Wizard

5. What is the evidence that the Good Witch sent Dorothy to the city?
   (A) A ring
   (B) Slippers
   (C) Buttons
   (D) Nothing

6. What does it mean when the doorman says "That's a horse of a different color"?
   (A) A horse is no more a fish than a whale is.
   (B) That makes matters even worse.
   (C) That changes the situation completely.
   (D) So many horses, so many colors.

Part 4 住民の歌を聞き、設問に答えなさい。　　　　　 18　Ⓢ 49

 エメラルドの国の住民は、毎日どんな暮らしをしているのだろうか。彼らの歌(♪
「これがオズの笑い方」) を聞いてみよう。

7. When do the people of the Emerald City get up?
   (A) At eleven
   (B) At noon
   (C) At one
   (D) At two

8. How long do they take for lunch?
   (A) Half an hour
   (B) One hour
   (C) Two hours
   (D) Several hours

9. How do they spend the day?
   (A) Busily
   (B) Quietly
   (C) Diligently
   (D) Pleasantly

Dictation

音声を聞き、適切な語句を空所に書き入れなさい。

Part 1

T2 14　S 45

1. (A) The man has grown a long (^{1}).

   (B) The man has a fine (^{2}).

   (C) The man is wearing a (^{3}) (^{4}).

   (D) The man is (^{5}) bald.

Part 2

T2 15-16　S 46-47

2. Would you (^{1}) (^{2}) to see the Wizard?

   (A) Oh, thank you so much.

   (B) Oh, but, but please. It's very (^{3}).

   (C) Well, yes, of course.

3. Dear! (^{4}) shall we do?

   (A) Well, (^{5}) (^{6}) hurry if we're going to see the Wizard.

   (B) It's the Witch! She's (^{7}) us here.

   (C) I've never seen a (^{8}) like that before.

Part 3

Doorman: Now, (¹   ) your (²   ).

Dorothy: We want to see the Wizard.

Doorman: Oh, oh…the Wizard? Ah…But nobody can see the Great Oz! Nobody's

ever seen the Great Oz! (³   ) (⁴   ) never seen him!

Dorothy: Well then, how do you know there is one?

Doorman: Because, he's . . . Oh . . . You're (⁵   ) my time!

Dorothy: Oh, please. Please, sir. (⁶   ) (⁷   ) (⁸   ) see the

Wizard. The Good Witch of the North (⁹   ) (¹⁰   ).

Doorman: Prove it!

Scarecrow: She's wearing the (¹¹   ) slippers she gave her!

Doorman: Oh, so she is! Well, (¹²   ) my (¹³   )! Why didn't

you say that in the first place? That's a horse of a different color!

Come on in!

Part 4

We get up at (¹   ) and start to work at (²   ). We (³   )

(⁴   ) (⁵   ) for lunch and then at (⁶   ) we're (⁷   ).

Jolly good fun! Ha-ha-ha, ho-ho-ho and (⁸   ) (⁹   ) (¹⁰   )

tra-la-las. That's how we (¹¹   ) the day away in the Merry Old Land of

Oz!

10. First I will take you to a little place
    _____ you can tidy up a bit.
    (A) when
    (B) where
    (C) what
    (D) how

11. We have been gone _____, and we feel so
    messy.
    (A) so a long time
    (B) a so long time
    (C) such a long time
    (D) a such long time

12. If you are Dorothy, that _____ a
    difference.
    (A) makes
    (B) takes
    (C) uses
    (D) raises

13. I can fairly hear my heart _____!
    (A) beats
    (B) to beat
    (C) beating
    (D) beaten

14. _____ another hour I will be King of the
    Forest.
    (A) By
    (B) At
    (C) In
    (D) Till

悪い魔女が描いた「飛行機雲」のメッセージに、エメラルドの国の住民たちは驚きパニックになってしまった。守衛は群がる人々に…

Here, here! Everything is all right. Stop fussing now;

everything is all right! The great and powerful Oz has got

matters well ---15---, I hope, and so you can all go home

and there is nothing ---16---. Get out ---17--- here now.

Go on! Go home! ---18--- can see the Great Oz!

15. (A) on foot
    (B) by heart
    (C) in hand
    (D) under arms

16. (A) worry about
    (B) to worry about
    (C) worrying
    (D) worried

17. (A) of
    (B) off
    (C) from
    (D) away

18. (A) Anybody
    (B) Somebody
    (C) Everybody
    (D) Nobody

ドロシーたちがエメラルドの都に到着した場面は、原作ではどのように描写され ているだろうか。映像と比較してみよう。

Even with eyes protected by the green spectacles, Dorothy and her friends were at first dazzled by the brilliancy of the wonderful City. The streets were lined with beautiful houses all built of green marble and studded everywhere with sparkling emeralds. They walked over a pavement of the same green marble, and where the blocks were joined together were rows of emeralds, set closely, and glittering in the brightness of the sun. —[1]—. The window panes were of green glass; even the sky above the City had a green tint, and the rays of the sun were green.

There were many people — men, women, and children — walking about, and these were all dressed in green clothes and had greenish skins. They looked at Dorothy and her strangely assorted company with wondering eyes, and the children all ran away and hid behind their mothers when they saw the Lion; but no one spoke to them. —[2]—. Green candy and green pop corn were offered for sale, as well as green shoes, green hats, and green clothes of all sorts. At one place a man was selling green lemonade, and when the children bought it Dorothy could see that they paid for it with green pennies.

There seemed to be no horses nor animals of any kind; the men carried things around in little green carts, which they pushed before them. —[3]—. Everyone seemed happy and contented and prosperous.

The Guardian of the Gates led them through the streets until they came to a big building, exactly in the middle of the City, which was the Palace of Oz, the Great Wizard. —[4]—. There was a soldier before the door, dressed in a green uniform and wearing a long green beard.

19. Which of the following is NOT found in the Emerald City?
    (A) houses
    (B) pavements
    (C) window panes
    (D) mice

20. What is true about the people in the City?
    (A) Nobody looks dissatisfied with life in the City.
    (B) Everyone stops to take a close look at Dorothy.
    (C) Children have no interest in Dorothy and her companions.
    (D) Mothers buy lemonade for their children.

21. What is NOT on sale?
    (A) candies
    (B) marbles
    (C) shoes
    (D) garments

22. What can be inferred about the Guardian of the Gates?
    (A) Wearing a green uniform, he guards the palace.
    (B) He hates his job, and wants to work inside the palace.
    (C) He carries Dorothy and her friends in a little green cart.
    (D) He takes Dorothy and her friends to the palace on foot.

23. In which of the positions marked [1], [2], [3] and [4] does the following sentence best belong?
    "Many shops stood in the street, and Dorothy saw that everything in them was green"
    (A) [1]
    (B) [2]
    (C) [3]
    (D) [4]

分詞

---

1. There's a law **protecting** folks from dogs that bite!

    （現在分詞・限定用法）

2. What if Dorothy keeps Toto **tied** up?

    （過去分詞・叙述用法）

3. The sun and wind had **changed** Aunt Em, too.

    （過去完了形）

4. Toto ran about the room, now here, now there, **barking** loudly.
    （分詞構文）

分詞には、現在分詞（一般に -ing 形）と過去分詞（一般に -en 形）があります。現在分詞は、進行形＜ be 動詞＋現在分詞＞の中で用いられ、過去分詞は、受動態＜ be 動詞＋過去分詞＞や、完了形＜ have (has, had) ＋過去分詞＞の中で用いられることもあれば、次の例に見るように、単独で、形容詞として用いられることもあります。

The progress in medicine is surprising.

I was surprised at the present.

現在分詞 surprising には「驚かせる」という能動的意味があり、過去分詞 surprised には「驚かされた」という受動的意味があります。

また、分詞は、次の例のように、Act 3 で学習した第 5 文型（S ＋ V ＋ O ＋ C）の C の位置にもよく使われ、直前の O（a man や his bicycle）を説明します。

We saw a man entering the house.

My son had his bicycle stolen yesterday.

さらに、分詞の導く語句が文に情報を添える働きをすることがあります。これを分詞構文といいます。分詞構文では、接続詞や主語などが省略されていると考えられますので、解釈するときは、それらを補う必要があります。

Exercises

（　　　）内から適切な語句を選びましょう。

1. We should not get too (excited / exciting) over such small things.

2. There was so much noise that I could not make myself (hearing / heard).

3. I was quite (pleased / pleasing) with the result.

4. (Written / Writing) in simple English, this book is easy to read.

5. Generally (speaking / spoken), people are happiest when enjoying life as it is.

ACT 9 You Must Prove Yourselves

 1:03:56-1:12:43

Words & Phrases

次の英単語・フレーズの意味を、下記の語群より選びなさい。 **T2** 22

1. ascend the throne （　）　　6. brochure （　）　　11. loyal （　）
2. graduate school （　）　　7. candidate （　）　　12. regal （　）
3. hippopotamus （　）　　8. fowl （　）　　13. rhyme （　）
4. rhinoceros （　）　　9. heel （　）　　14. sparrow （　）
5. transparent （　）　　10. legal （　）　　15. supposing （　）

a. 王の　　　d. かかと　　　g. 大学院　　　j. 韻（を踏む）　　　m. もし〜ならば
b. カバ　　　e. 候補者　　　h. 透明な　　　k. 王位に就く　　　n. 忠誠な、誠実な
c. サイ　　　f. スズメ　　　i. 家禽、鳥　　　l. パンフレット　　　o. 法律の、適法な

Listening Tips

子音の聞き取り（1）

　口腔内のどこかで呼気の流れが阻害される子音は、<u>どこで空気の流れが阻害される</u>のか（調音点）、<u>どのようにどの程度阻害されるのか</u>（調音方法）、声帯の振動を伴う有声音なのか声帯の振動を伴わない無声音なのか、などの観点で分類されます。

　Exercises では 3 つの無声摩擦音を取り上げます。/s/（歯茎摩擦音）は舌の前面を上歯茎に近づけ、その隙間から息を鋭く押し出します。/ʃ/（硬口蓋摩擦音）は、/s/に比べて舌が上あごに接する範囲が大きく、舌全体がやや後ろ寄りとなります。日本語の「シ」よりも強い摩擦を伴います。/θ/（歯間摩擦音）は、舌全体を平らにして上前歯の後ろから舌先を滑り出して発音します。/θ/ や /ð/ はいわゆる th の音ですが、they /ðeɪ/ を「上下の歯で舌先を噛む」と摩擦音ではなく閉鎖音 /d/ のようになってしまい day /deɪ/ と聞こえてしまいますので、噛んではいけないということに十分注意しましょう。

Exercises ──────────────── **T2** 23 **S** 50

音声を聞いて、発音されているものに○をつけましょう。

1. /s/ /ʃ/ /θ/　　a. /s/ /ʃ/ /θ/　　b. /s/ /ʃ/ /θ/　　c. /s/ /ʃ/ /θ/　　d. /s/ /ʃ/ /θ/

2. /s/ /ʃ/　　a. see she　　b. see she　　c. sell shell　　d. sell shell

3. /s/ /θ/　　a. sink think　　b. sink think　　c. worse worth　　d. worse worth

Part 1　写真の場面を最も適切に表している音声を選びなさい。　 24 Ⓢ 51

1. Ⓐ Ⓑ Ⓒ Ⓓ

Part 2　問いかけに対する最も適切な応答を選びなさい。　25-26 Ⓢ 52-53

 いよいよオズの魔法使いに会えるかもしれないというときに、急にライオンが外で待っていると言い出す。かかしはブリキ男に…

2. Ⓐ Ⓑ Ⓒ

 オズの魔法使いはドロシーたちの欲しがっているものを全て与えてやるという。しかし無条件でというわけにはいかないようだ。

3. Ⓐ Ⓑ Ⓒ

Part 3　会話を聞き、設問に答えなさい。　 27 Ⓢ 54

（登場話者：Dorothy, Lion, Tin Man）

 守衛はドロシーたちのことを魔法使いに伝えに行った。ライオンはもうすぐ勇気がもらえると大喜び。浮かれるライオンにドロシーは…

4. What does Lion mean when he says "Imposseros!"?
　(A) It is impolite.
　(B) It is important.
　(C) It is impossible.
　(D) It is imported.

5. Why does Lion use the phrase "from top to bottomus"?
   (A) He loves hippopotami very much.
   (B) He wants to use a word that rhymes with "hippopotamus."
   (C) He is terribly afraid of hippopotamuses.
   (D) He wishes he were a hippopotamus.

6. What does Lion say he will do when he meets an elephant?
   (A) He will run away from the elephant as fast as possible.
   (B) He will cover the elephant in transparent wrapping.
   (C) He will hit the elephant quickly several times.
   (D) He will allow the elephant to ascend the throne.

Part 4 ライオンの歌の歌詞を聞き、設問に答えなさい。　 28　 55

オズの魔法使いが自分に勇気をくれると信じるライオンは、もうすぐ森の王様に
なれると喜び歌う（♪「もしも勇気があったなら」）。

7. What would Lion wear if he were King?
   (A) A smooth shiny robe
   (B) A black legal garment
   (C) A quick-drying shirt
   (D) A pair of water-proof shoes

8. What does Lion say he will do to fish or fowl?
   (A) He will eat them up.
   (B) He will give them orders.
   (C) He will chase them away.
   (D) He will be loyal to them.

9. How would the trees and mountains react if Lion clicked his heels?
   (A) They would crumble to the sea.
   (B) They would show little interest in him.
   (C) They would show respect to him.
   (D) They would be angry with his behavior.

Dictation

音声を聞き、適切な語句を空所に書き入れなさい。

Part 1

⑫ 24 Ⓢ 51

1. (A) Tin Man is (^{1}).

   (B) Lion is pulling his (^{2}) (^{3}).

   (C) Scarecrow is running away.

   (D) They are all walking (^{4}) (^{5}) (^{6}).

Part 2

⑫ 25-26 Ⓢ 52-53

2. What's the (^{1}) (^{2}) Lion?

   (A) You can (^{3}) (^{4}) (^{5}).

   (B) Oh, he's just scared again.

   (C) I'd be too scared to ask him for it.

3. To prove yourselves worthy, bring me the broomstick of the Witch of the West.

   (A) A while (^{6}), we were walking down the Yellow Brick Road.

   (B) But if we do that, we'll have to kill her to get it!

   (C) Did you bring your broomstick (^{7}) (^{8})?

Part 3

Dorothy: Your Majesty, if you were King, you wouldn't be afraid of anything?

Lion: Not nobody. Not nohow.

Tin Man: Not even a (^{1})?

Lion: Imposseros!

Dorothy: How about a (^{2})?

Lion: Why, I'd (^{3}) him from (^{4}) to bottomus!

Dorothy: Supposing you met (^{5}) (^{6})?

Lion: I'd wrap him up in cellophant.

Part 4

If I were King of the Forest, not (^{1}), not (^{2}), not

(^{3}), my regal (^{4}) of the forest would be (^{5}), not

(^{6}), not chintz. I'd command each thing, be it fish or (^{7}),

with a woof and a woof, and a (^{8}) growl . . . woof. As I'd (^{9})

my (^{10}), all the trees would (^{11}), and the mountains (^{12}),

and the (^{13}) kowtow, and the (^{14}) would take wing, if I

were King!

10. It looks like we came a long way for
    _____.
    (A) vain
    (B) waste
    (C) idle
    (D) nothing

11. I was so happy. I thought I was _____
    my way home.
    (A) at
    (B) in
    (C) of
    (D) on

12. The Great and Powerful Oz knows _____
    you have come.
    (A) why
    (B) what
    (C) when
    (D) which

13. You dare _____ to me for a heart, do you?
    (A) coming
    (B) to come
    (C) came
    (D) have come

14. Bring me her broomstick _____ I will
    grant your requests.
    (A) if
    (B) or
    (C) and
    (D) though

守衛は、ドロシーたちには会わないからすぐに帰れというオズの魔法使いの言葉を伝える。ドロシーは泣き出して…

Auntie Em was so good to me, and I never ---15--- it.

Running away and hurting her feelings . . . Professor

Marvel said she was sick. She may ---16---, and it's

all my ---17---. Oh, I'll never ---18--- myself! Never,

never, never!

15. (A) applied
    (B) approached
    (C) appreciated
    (D) appointed

16. (A) be dying
    (B) death
    (C) dyeing
    (D) dead

17. (A) fault
    (B) failure
    (C) responsible
    (D) faulty

18. (A) allow
    (B) permit
    (C) forgive
    (D) admit

最近は往年の名画がリバイバル上映される機会も多くなった。上映会に行く相談をするメールのやり取りを読んでみよう。

Hi Shizuka,

　　　It's been a while. How are you doing? I was hoping you'd come to see a movie with me this weekend. There's a classic movie festival in town (poster attached). I've actually seen these films before, and they're all really good. My favorite is *Casablanca*. I could talk about it for hours. The one starring Audrey Hepburn is about a series of murders, and is really thrilling. *The Third Man* is pretty good too. The guy in the picture is the legendary Orson Welles. I know you're studying *The Wonderful Wizard of Oz* at graduate school, so maybe you want to see the film version.

　　　Think about it and let me know if you want to go and what you'd like to see. It would be great to see you again!

Best,
Mark

Ingrid Bergman　Humphrey Bogart
Casablanca
1942 black and white

Alida Valli　Joseph Cotten　Orson Welles
The Third Man
1963 black and white

Audrey Hepburn　Cary Grant
Charade
1963 color

Judy Garland
The Wizard of Oz
1939 color

CLASSIC MOVIE FESTIVAL
October 3-10, 2020
Stellar Cinema Theater, Yurakucho

Admission: Adults ¥1,300　Children ¥800　Two-Ticket Package ¥2,500

Showtimes:	*Casablanca*	*Charade*	*The Third Man*	*The Wizard of Oz*
	Oct 3 Sat, Oct 7 Wed	Oct 4 Sun, Oct 8 Thu	Oct 5 Mon, Oct 9 Fri	Oct 6 Tue, Oct 10 Sat

Shows daily at 10:00, 14:00, and 17:00

Hi Mark,

Good to hear from you. I'd love to see one of the films with you. Actually, I don't enjoy black and white films. They tend to be too dark and the subtitles are hard to read. Another thing, Audrey Hepburn is my favorite actress, but I usually shy away from scary thrillers with violent scenes. So you can probably guess which one of the films I want to see.   Can you get the tickets?

By the way, I wouldn't mind having lunch together someplace nice before the film. I'll tell you everything I know about the story. I've studied it extensively, so you'll get a two-hour lecture ;-)   Looking forward to seeing you this weekend.

Best,
Shizuka

19. What is attached to the first email?
   (A) A brochure
   (B) An advertisement
   (C) A ticket
   (D) A seat map

20. Who stars in Mark's favorite film?
   (A) Humphrey Bogart
   (B) Orson Welles
   (C) Audrey Hepburn
   (D) Judy Garland

21. How much will Mark pay for the tickets?
   (A) ¥1,300
   (B) ¥1,600
   (C) ¥2,500
   (D) ¥2,600

22. What is Shizuka probably studying at grad school?
   (A) Tourism and hospitality
   (B) American literature
   (C) Applied chemistry
   (D) Global economy

23. Which movie are they going to see?
   (A) *Charade* at 10:00 on October 3
   (B) *Charade* at 14:00 on October 4
   (C) *The Third Man* at 17:00 on October 9
   (D) *The Wizard of Oz* at 14:00 on October 10

比較

---

1. It's on the door, **as plain as** the nose on my face!
2. Dorothy's eyes grew **bigger** and **bigger** at the wonderful sights she saw.
3. Happiness is **the best** thing in the world.

　形容詞や副詞は程度の差を表すために形を変えます。これを比較変化といい、原級、比較級、最上級の 3 つがあります。ここで、主な比較表現を確認しておきましょう。

原級（辞書の見出しの形）による比較表現

as ＋原級＋ as ...	…と同じぐらい〜
X times as ＋原級＋ as ...	…の X 倍の〜
as ＋原級＋ as one can (could) as ＋原級＋ as possible	できるだけ〜

比較級（原級＋ -er または more ＋原級）による比較表現

比較級 ＋ than ...	…よりも〜
the ＋ 比較級 ＋ of the two	2 つのうち、より〜のほう
the ＋ 比較級 , the ＋ 比較級	…すればするほど〜

最上級（原級＋ -est または most ＋原級）による比較表現

the ＋ 最上級 ＋ of (in) ...	…の中で最も〜
the ＋ X（序数）＋ 最上級 ＋ ...	X 番目に〜な…

※ tall や small などの原級の意味を強めたい場合は very tall や very small となるが、taller や smaller などの比較級を強調するときは前に much / even / far がついて much taller, even smaller などとなり、very を用いることはできない。

Exercises

(　　　) 内から適切な語句を選びましょう。

1. She speaks as (many / much) as ten languages.

2. He decided to employ the (smarter / smartest) of the two candidates.

3. This book is three times (thicker / thickest) than that one.

4. She is senior (to / than) her husband in the workplace.

5. "How do you feel now?" "I feel (much / very) better, thank you."

Act 10 The Witch's Castle

 1:12:43-1:20:10

Words & Phrases

次の英単語・フレーズの意味を、下記の語群より選びなさい。 **T2** 32

1. abandon	( )	6. commentary	( )	11. jam	( )	
2. aid	( )	7. enthusiastic	( )	12. masterpiece	( )	
3. brand-new	( )	8. flock	( )	13. representative	( )	
4. chest	( )	9. generation	( )	14. ridiculous	( )	
5. companion	( )	10. insect	( )	15. spell	( )	

a. 援助、支援　　d. 昆虫　　　　g. 世代　　　j. 熱狂的な　　m. 見捨てる
b. 胸、胸部　　　e. 雑踏、渋滞　h. 代表者　　　k. ばかげた　　n. 呪文、まじない
c. 傑作、名作　　f. 群れをなす　i. 仲間、連れ　l. 真新しい　　o. 論評、実況解説

Listening Tips

子音の聞き取り（2）

　Exercises の問題 1 の light の /l/（歯茎側音）は舌先をしっかりと上歯茎に接触させ、舌の両脇を気流が通り抜けます。right の /r/（歯茎半母音）は、舌先がどこにも触れない代わりに、舌の奥の両脇が上の奥歯の歯茎に接します。問題 2 と 3 は、/v/, /f/, /b/ の 3 つの音に関する設問です。/v/ と /f/（唇歯摩擦音）は、下唇の内側を上の前歯に押し当て、その隙間を気流が通ります。摩擦音 /v/ と /f/ を発音するときに、上の歯で下唇を噛んではいけません。摩擦音（/v/ と /f/）の発音は、長く継続させることができますが、/b/（両唇閉鎖音）はとじ合わせられた上下の唇が開放されるときに音が生まれる瞬間の音です。継続している /v/, /f/（摩擦音）か、瞬間の /b/（閉鎖音）かを聞き分けるとよいでしょう。また、leave /liːv/ と leaf /liːf/ の聞き分けは、母音の長さの違いも手がかりになります。有声音 /v/ が後続する /iː/（つまり leave）の方が、無声音 /f/ が後続する /iː/（つまり leaf）よりも長く発音されます。

Exercises ──────────────── **T2** 33 **S** 56

音声を聞いて、発音されているものに○をつけましょう。

1. /l/ /r/	a. light right	b. light right	c. flight fright	d. flight fright
2. /v/ /b/	a. very berry	b. very berry	c. vest best	d. vest best
3. /v/ /f/	a. vase face	b. vase face	c. leave leaf	d. leave leaf

Part 1 写真の場面を最も適切に表している音声を選びなさい。　🔊 34　Ⓢ 57

1. Ⓐ Ⓑ Ⓒ Ⓓ

Part 2 問いかけに対する最も適切な応答を選びなさい。　🔊35-36　Ⓢ 58-59

魔女の城に向かう一行は、幽霊の森 (Haunted Forest) に差し掛かる。いかにもお化け (spooks) が出そうな雰囲気に、かかしは…

2. Ⓐ Ⓑ Ⓒ

ドロシーとトトは羽のある猿たちにさらわれて魔女の城に連れてこられてしまった。愛犬トトを魔女にとられたドロシーは…

3. Ⓐ Ⓑ Ⓒ

Part 3 会話を聞き、設問に答えなさい。　🔊 37　Ⓢ 60
（登場話者：Scarecrow, Tin Man, Lion）

ドロシーたちが幽霊の森で羽のある猿たちの襲撃を受けた直後の、ライオン、ブリキ男、かかしの会話を聞いてみよう。

4. What happened to Scarecrow?
   (A) He was given first aid.
   (B) He was filled with fresh straw.
   (C) He hurt himself.
   (D) He was torn apart.

5. What is the meaning of the idiomatic expression "knock the stuffing out of"?
   (A) To take the straw stuffing out of someone
   (B) To make someone feel strong and powerful
   (C) To cause someone to suffer a heavy defeat
   (D) To beat someone to death

6. What will Tin Man, Lion, and Scarecrow do next?
   (A) They will sit down and discuss what they should do.
   (B) They will put up with the pain in their chests.
   (C) They will search for Scarecrow's heart.
   (D) They will look for missing Dorothy.

Part 4 悪い魔女の話を聞き、設問に答えなさい。　

不気味で陰鬱な幽霊の森の空気は、悪い魔女の演出だったようだ。魔女は羽のある猿のボスを呼び出して、ある命令をする。

7. What does the Wicked Witch order the leader of the winged monkeys to do?
   (A) Fly to the Haunted Forest by himself
   (B) Do good to the girl and the dog
   (C) Do harm to the girl and the dog
   (D) Get the girl and her dog back safe and sound

8. What does the Witch say to the leader about Scarecrow, Tin Man, and Lion?
   (A) His army must not hurt or injure them.
   (B) His army should stay away from them.
   (C) He should be careful of them.
   (D) He can do whatever he likes with them.

9. What does the Witch want most?
   (A) Ruby necklaces
   (B) The shoes the girl is wearing
   (C) The girl's little dog
   (D) The girl's companions

Dictation

音声を聞き、適切な語句を空所に書き入れなさい。

Part 1

🅣 34 Ⓢ 57

1. (A) Tin Man and Lion are (^{1}) (^{2}) the hillside.

  (B) Tin Man is cutting Lion's (^{3}).

  (C) Tin Man is holding on to Lion's (^{4})

  (D) Tin Man and Lion are (^{5}) each other.

Part 2

🅣 35-36 Ⓢ 58-59

2. I believe there are spooks around here.

  (A) That's (^{1})! That's (^{2}).

  (B) What a nice little dog.

  (C) I'm trying to (^{3}) (^{4}) to you.

3. What are you going to do with my dog? Give him (^{5}) to me!

  (A) All in (^{6}) (^{7}), my pretty.

  (B) I'm sorry I didn't.

  (C) Oh, don't go away!

Part 3

Scarecrow: Help! Help! Help!

Tin Man: Oh, well. What (^{1}) (^{2}) you?

Scarecrow: They (^{3}) my (^{4}) (^{5}), and they threw them

over there! Then they took my (^{6}) (^{7}) and they

threw it over there!

Tin Man: Well, that's you all over!

Lion: They sure knocked the (^{8}) (^{9}) (^{10}) you,

didn't they?

Scarecrow: Don't stand there talking! Put me (^{11})! We've got to find

Dorothy!

Part 4

Take your (^{1}) to the (^{2}) Forest, and bring me Dorothy

and her dog. Do what you like with the Scarecrow, the Tin Man, and the Lion,

but I want her (^{3}) and (^{4})! They'll give you (^{5})

(^{6}). I promise you that. I've sent a little (^{7}) (^{8})

(^{9}) to take the fight out of them. Ha ha ha ha! Take (^{10})

(^{11}) of those ruby slippers. I want those (^{12}) (^{13}) (^{14}).

Now fly! Fly!

10. I do _____ in spooks.
    (A) feel
    (B) think
    (C) believe
    (D) regard

11. It is so kind _____ you to visit me in my loneliness.
    (A) to
    (B) of
    (C) in
    (D) for

12. You have been more trouble to me _____ you are worth, one way or another.
    (A) of
    (B) well
    (C) to
    (D) than

13. That is _____ much longer you have got to be alive, and it is not long!
    (A) how
    (B) so
    (C) very
    (D) many

14. Oh, I hope my strength _____ out.
    (A) continues
    (B) lasts
    (C) holds
    (D) keeps

 とうとうドロシーを捕まえた悪い魔女。彼女の狙いはドロシーの履いている靴にあった。靴を脱がそうとする魔女だが、うまくいかず…

Fool ---15--- I am! I should have remembered.

Those slippers will never come off, as ---16--- as

you are alive. But that is not ---17--- is worrying

me. It is how to do it. These things must ---18---

delicately, or you hurt the spell!

15. (A) what
    (B) whose
    (C) to whom
    (D) that

16. (A) long
    (B) soon
    (C) far
    (D) much

17. (A) that
    (B) what
    (C) which
    (D) it

18. (A) have done
    (B) be done
    (C) do
    (D) be doing

『ニューヨークタイムズ』に掲載された初演の広告（上）と『デイリーニュース』
紙のレビュー（下）から当時の人々の様子に触れてみよう。

New York Times, August 15, 1939

Review: 'The Wizard of Oz' is an instant classic

Oh, to be at the Capitol, now that "Oz" is here, must have been the dearest wish of New Yorkers yesterday. A goodly number of the population turned out to see the first showing of the picture and the jam around the theatre kept the police busy from the time the line began to form at 6 A.M. on through the day.

The crowds flocked to the Capitol to see the long-heralded Metro-Goldwyn-Mayer film version of the famous Baum stories and to welcome the little star of the picture, Judy Garland, who is making personal appearances with the irrepressible Mickey Rooney, on the stage.

It was an enthusiastic and friendly throng for whom Judy and Mickey sang and danced with all the verve and rhythmic bounce of youth. The audience was enthusiastic about the picture, which is a delightful fantasy of the "Snow White and Seven Dwarfs" type. Real people, of course, represent the leading characters of the L. Frank Baum stories, on which the film is based, and which gave pleasure to children for several generations.

https://www.nydailynews.com/entertainment/movies/wizard-oz-instant-disney-classic-1939-review-article-1.2330990

Notes:

irrepressible 「快活な、活発な」 throng 「群衆、人だかり」 verve 「力強さ、活力」

dwarf 「こびと、ドワーフ」

19. When in 1939 was the review published?
    (A) August 15
    (B) August 16
    (C) August 17
    (D) August 18

20. What happened on the first day of screening?
    (A) People queued up all day long at the theater.
    (B) Judy Garland gave a detailed commentary about the film.
    (C) "Snow White" was shown together with "The Wizard of Oz."
    (D) The theater opened earlier than usual.

21. What is true about Mickey Rooney?
    (A) He sang and danced in "The Wizard of Oz."
    (B) He directed "Snow White and Seven Dwarfs."
    (C) He came to the Capitol to entertain the audience.
    (D) He was the CEO of Metro-Goldwyn-Mayer.

22. In the title of the review, the phrase "an instant classic" is closest in meaning to:
    (A) a movie which was filmed long ago but is released now
    (B) a picture which has immediately been recognized as a masterpiece
    (C) an artwork which was produced in a very short period of time
    (D) a commercial film which includes various classical music

23. According to the review, what is true about the showing of the picture?
    (A) A large portion of the audience was children.
    (B) Selected fans could shake hands with Judy Garland on stage.
    (C) People were entertained by Judy Garland as well as the film.
    (D) Some of the people who lined up were kept outside by the police.

Grammar Training

接続詞

---

1. Witches are old **and** ugly. （等位接続詞）

2. Are you a good witch **or** a bad witch? （等位接続詞）

3. **When** I gain those ruby slippers, my power will be the greatest in Oz! （従位接続詞）

4. Dorothy noticed **that** the house was not moving. （名詞節を導く接続詞）

　接続詞は、語と語、句と句、節（文）と節（文）のような、同じ要素を連結する働きをします。また、that や whether のような接続詞は名詞節を導き、その節全体が主語・目的語・補語の役割を果たします。代表的な接続詞の用法と意味を確認しましょう。

語と語、句と句、節と節を対等に結びつける等位接続詞
　　and「…と〜」、but「…だが〜」、or「…か〜」

節と節を結びつけ、主節を修飾する従属節を導く従位接続詞
　　when「〜する時に」、before「〜する前に」、after「〜した後に」、while「〜している間に」、until「〜するまで」、since「〜して以来、〜なので」、because「〜なので」、if「もし〜であれば」、unless「もし〜しなければ」、although (though)「〜だけれども」、as soon as「〜するとすぐ」、by the time「〜する時までに」

名詞節を導く接続詞
　　that「〜ということ」、whether「〜かどうか」、if「〜かどうか」

Exercises

（　　）内から適切な語句を選びましょう。

1. Susan will have finished her homework (by / until) then.

2. Our son doesn't have a car (and / or) a bike.

3. (Although / However) I have my own car, I prefer to travel by train.

4. A book is not always good just (because / since) it was written by a famous scholar.

5. You can read a magazine (during / while) you wait for your turn.

6. My success depends on (if / whether) or not you give me a hand.

7. Our flight was cancelled (because of / despite) the thick fog.

Act 11 Go in There for Dorothy

 1:20:10-1:27:32

Words & Phrases

次の英単語・フレーズの意味を、下記の語群より選びなさい。　　　　　T2 42

1. analogy　　　　（　　）　6. hourglass　　　　（　　）　11. discrimination　（　　）
2. continuous　　（　　）　7. integrate　　　　（　　）　12. significance　　（　　）
3. deceive　　　　（　　）　8. prejudice　　　　（　　）　13. squeak　　　　（　　）
4. descend　　　　（　　）　9. prosperity　　　　（　　）　14. surrender　　　（　　）
5. diversity　　　（　　）　10. signify　　　　　（　　）　15. sympathy　　　（　　）

a.　継続的な　　　d.　砂時計　　　g.　重要性、意義　　j.　統合する　　　m.　降りる、下る
b.　降伏する　　　e.　だます　　　h.　偏見、先入観　　k.　同情、共感　　n.　キーキー音を立てる
c.　差別　　　　　f.　多様性　　　i.　類推、共通点　　l.　繁栄、成功　　o.　示す、意味する

Listening Tips

さまざまな英語の発音

　ドロシーが飼い犬「トト」に向かって "Toto" と呼びかけるときの発音を注意深く聞くと、最初の /t/ と 2 つ目の /t/ の発音が違うことに気がつきます。2 つ目の /t/ は /d/ のような音色を帯びています。これはアメリカ英語の特徴の一つで、母音に挟まれた /t/ が有声化しています（この発音は [t̬] という記号で表します）。アメリカ英語とイギリス英語の発音の最も大きな違いは、アメリカ英語では car /kɑːr/, bird /bɚːd (bɝːd)/ のように母音が r 音を帯びている (rhotic, r-colored) のに対して、イギリス英語では car /kɑː/, bird /bəːd (bɜːd)/ と発音されることです。また、schedule などアメリカ英語とイギリス英語では発音そのものが全く違っていたり、íce crèam（米）と ice créam（英）などアクセントが違っていたりする場合もあります。TOEIC では、アメリカ英語、イギリス英語、オーストラリア英語などさまざまな英語の発音が聞かれますので、変異形 (variant) の代表的なものは知っておくとよいでしょう。

Exercises ──────────────── T2 43 S 62 ─

次の単語について、それぞれどのような発音の変異形があるかを調べ、発音しましょう。

1. advertisement [　　　　　　　]　4. often　　[　　　　　　　　　]
2. data　　　　　[　　　　　　　]　5. schedule [　　　　　　　　　]
3. either　　　　[　　　　　　　]　6. tomato　 [　　　　　　　　　]

Part 1 写真の場面を最も適切に表している音声を選びなさい。 ⏱44 ⓢ63

1. Ⓐ Ⓑ Ⓒ Ⓓ

Part 2 問いかけに対する最も適切な応答を選びなさい。 ⏱45-46 ⓢ64-65

 かかしが火をつけられたためドロシーが水をかけると、その水が魔女にもかかり、溶けて死んでしまう。衛兵はドロシーに…

2. Ⓐ Ⓑ Ⓒ

 2に続く場面。死んでしまった魔女のそばに、ほうきが残されている。それを見てドロシーが衛兵に言う台詞。

3. Ⓐ Ⓑ Ⓒ

Part 3 会話を聞き、設問に答えなさい。 ⏱47 ⓢ66
（登場話者：Scarecrow, Lion, Dorothy）

 ライオン、かかし、ブリキ男はドロシーを救い出すために魔女の城に潜入した。三人は閉じ込められているドロシーに声をかけるが…

4. What does Scarecrow want to make certain?
   (A) He can really break down the door.
   (B) Dorothy is really behind the door.
   (C) He can lock Dorothy in the room.
   (D) Dorothy can clearly hear them calling her.

5. Why is Dorothy in haste?

    (A) She locked herself out of the room.

    (B) She cannot fight on an empty stomach.

    (C) She does not have much time left.

    (D) She cannot turn over the hourglass.

6. What is most likely to happen next?

    (A) The door will be forced open.

    (B) Dorothy will be deserted.

    (C) Everybody will stay in the room.

    (D) The hourglass will be destroyed.

Part 4 ライオンの話を聞き、設問に答えなさい。　　　 48　 67

ライオン、かかし、ブリキ男はドロシーがとらわれている魔女の城にやってきた。
いよいよ救出作戦にかかるというときのライオンの台詞。

7. What does Lion say he will do to the guards?

    (A) Surrender to them

    (B) Persuade them

    (C) Beat them up

    (D) Join them

8. Why is Lion worried?

    (A) He may not find Dorothy.

    (B) He may be imprisoned.

    (C) He may be killed.

    (D) He may not arrive in time.

9. What does Lion mean when he says "Talk me out of it"?

    (A) He is confident of his victory.

    (B) He really does not want to go.

    (C) He is proud of his courage.

    (D) He wants to discuss the plan with his friends.

Dictation

音声を聞き、適切な語句を空所に書き入れなさい。

Part 1

1. (A) The girls are walking hand in hand.

   (B) The guards are (¹   ) in a line.

   (C) The guards are carrying (²   ).

   (D) The garden (³   ) (⁴   ) (⁵   ) visitors.

Part 2

2. (¹   ) (²   ). You've killed her.

   (A) I knew you would!

   (B) I wouldn't (³   ) (⁴   ) (⁵   ).

   (C) I didn't (⁶   ) (⁷   ) kill her.

3. The (⁸   )! May we have it?

   (A) Please. And take it with you.

   (B) Oh, thank you so much!

   (C) No, you don't.

Part 3

Scarecrow: Wait! We'd better (^{1}) (^{2}). Dorothy, are you in there?

Lion: It's us!

Dorothy: Yes! It's me! She's (^{3}) (^{4}) (^{5}).

Lion: Listen, fellows. It's her. We have got to (^{6}) (^{7}) (^{8})! Open the door!

Dorothy: Oh, hurry! Please hurry! The (^{9}) is (^{10}) (^{11})!

Lion: Get back.

Part 4

All right, I'll go in there for Dorothy, Wicked Witch or no Wicked Witch, guards or no guards. I'll (^{1}) (^{2}) (^{3}). Ohhh! I may not (^{4}) (^{5}) (^{6}), but I'm going in there. There is only (^{7}) (^{8}) I want you (^{9}) to do. Talk me (^{10}) (^{11}) (^{12}).

10. Oh, I hate to _____ of her in there. We have got to get her out!
    (A) think
    (B) regard
    (C) consider
    (D) believe

11. Do not cry now. We have not got the oil can with us and you have been squeaking _____.
    (A) as it is
    (B) as it were
    (C) so forth
    (D) so to speak

12. I have got a plan for _____ to get in there.
    (A) as
    (B) which
    (C) how
    (D) where

13. Lion! I knew you _____.
    (A) are coming
    (B) will come
    (C) will have come
    (D) would come

14. Hurry, we have got _____ time to lose.
    (A) no
    (B) few
    (C) any
    (D) every

Part 6 次の英文の空所に入る最も適切な語句を選びなさい。

 2 の直前のシーン。ドロシーに水をかけられた魔女が溶けて死んでいくときの断末魔の叫びである。

No, don't throw that water! Ohhhhh! You cursed brat!

Look ---15--- you have done! I'm melting! I'm melting!

Oh, what a world! What a world! Who ---16--- a good

little girl like you could destroy my beautiful ---17---?

Ohhhhh! Look out! Look out! I'm ---18---. Ohhhhh!

[*dies*]

15. (A) that
    (B) what
    (C) out
    (D) at

16. (A) think
    (B) are thought
    (C) would be thought
    (D) would have thought

17. (A) wick
    (B) wicked
    (C) wickedly
    (D) wickedness

18. (A) go
    (B) went
    (C) going
    (D) having gone

作品を代表する楽曲 "Over the Rainbow" に見られる重要なイメージ、虹に
ついて書かれたエッセイを読んでみよう。

Throughout history, people have assigned spiritual significance to the mysterious beauty of rainbows. In the Bible, the rainbow is a message from God promising Noah there will be no more Floods. In Nordic myth, the gods in the sky reach Earth by traveling on a rainbow bridge. In ancient Japanese texts, it is written that the god Izanagi and goddess Izanami descended to earth on a "floating bridge of heaven," that is, a rainbow.

Since then, science has shown us what rainbows actually are. In the seventeenth century, Isaac Newton proved that white light was made of a continuous spectrum of colors. He defined these as red, orange, yellow, green, blue, indigo, and violet: seven colors by analogy with the seven notes in the musical scale. Today, we learn these in school as the seven colors of the rainbow.

In recent times, the rainbow has taken on a new meaning as a symbol of the fight to defend the rights of sexual minorities, also called LGBT (lesbian, gay, bisexual, and transgender). Since 1978, the Rainbow Flag has been carried at Gay Pride parades; and even more recently, on social networks, people overlay rainbows on their profile pictures to signify support for LGBT rights. In Japan, events in support of LGBT rights have used the symbol in their name, notably Rainbow Festa! and Tokyo Rainbow Pride.

How did the rainbow come to be established as an LGBT emblem? Could there be a connection with the iconic song "Over the Rainbow" from the film *The Wizard of Oz*? In this song, as in ancient myths, the rainbow represents a bridge between the real world and an ideal place: Dorothy dreams of leaving her difficult life in Kansas to go to a problem-free land beyond the rainbow. LGBT people who suffer because of prejudice may also dream of an ideal society free from discrimination. Furthermore, long after Judy Garland played Dorothy in the movie, she continued to sing *"Over the Rainbow"* in live performances. She became an icon of the LGBT community. In fact, at a time when it was still a crime to be homosexual in America, gay people would ask each other if they were a "friend of Dorothy" as a secret way to find out each other's sexual orientation. Perhaps the strong association with the song and with Garland helped establish the rainbow as an emblem for gay rights.

Newton's scientific discovery gave us a symbol of diversity: white light made up of an array of colors. Our society is also made up of diverse people, including people with different sexual orientations. Isn't ignoring sexual and gender minorities like trying to remove a color from the rainbow? Discrimination has existed throughout history, but little by little humanity is finding ways to move beyond it. If we accept sexual diversity, we make our society stronger, integrating all its "colors." Surely, this is not merely a dream of a land "over the rainbow," but a very real improvement to our community.

Notes:

Noah「ノア」箱舟で知られる『創世記』中の人物。**Nordic**「北欧の」**Isaac Newton**「アイザック・ニュートン」万有引力の法則を発見した物理学者・数学者。**spectrum**「スペクトル」太陽光をプリズムで分解したときに得られる連続した色帯。**overlay**「上に重ねる」

19. What did ancient people regard rainbows as?
    (A) A warning of natural disaster
    (B) A bridge for the dead to go to heaven
    (C) A sign of wealth and prosperity
    (D) Something sacred that connects gods and people

20. Which of the following is NOT included in the seven colors of the rainbow?
    (A) Red
    (B) Blue
    (C) White
    (D) Green

21. What has the rainbow become associated with?
    (A) Recognition of sexual diversity
    (B) The fight against racial discrimination
    (C) Pride in one's origin and nationality
    (D) The ubiquity of Social Networking Services

22. What did a "friend of Dorothy" mean?
    (A) A character in *The Wizard of Oz*
    (B) A great fan of Judy Garland
    (C) A gay person
    (D) A heterosexual person

23. According to the passage, what does the discovery of the spectrum of light symbolize?
    (A) Light is composed of only seven colors.
    (B) Scientific findings improve our quality of life.
    (C) A society free from discrimination is merely a dream.
    (D) Our community is at its best when it integrates everyone.

関係詞

---

1. Munchkins are the little people **who** live in this land.
2. The dreams **that** you dare to dream really do come true.
3. It really was no miracle. **What** happened was just this.
4. The great and powerful Oz knows **why** you have come.

　関係詞は、名詞を後ろから修飾する形容詞節を導く要素で、代名詞の役割を果たすものを関係代名詞、副詞の役割を果たすものを関係副詞と呼びます。

　関係代名詞は、表1のように、修飾される名詞（先行詞）の種類と、関係代名詞の文法的機能によって、どの形式が使われるのかが決まっています。

　関係副詞は、時・場所・理由・方法を表す名詞を修飾し、表2のように、先行詞の種類によってそれぞれ異なる関係副詞が使われます（ただし、方法を表す場合、先行詞の the way か関係副詞の how のどちらかが必ず省略されます）。どの環境でどの関係代名詞や関係副詞が使われるのかを、下の表で確認しましょう。

表1　さまざまな関係代名詞

		文法的機能		
		主格	所有格	目的格
先行詞	人	who	whose	whom (who)
	人以外	which	whose	which
	人・人以外	that	—	that
	先行詞を含む	what	—	what

表2　さまざまな関係副詞

先行詞	時を表わす語	場所を表わす語	reason（理由）	way（方法）
関係副詞	when	where	why	how

Exercises

（　　）内から適切な語句を選びましょう。

1. Susan married a man (who / whom) everybody had thought was Lucy's boyfriend.

2. A friend (who / whom) I thought to be honest deceived me.

3. (That / What) seems easy at first often turns out to be difficult.

4. We moved to London, (when / where) we lived for three years.

5. Autumn is (when / where) children go back to school in America.

Act 12 Lost and Found

 1:27:32-1:41:42

Words & Phrases

次の英単語・フレーズの意味を、下記の語群より選びなさい。　　　　　　📺 52

1. backyard	( )	6. desire	( )	11. sentimental	( )
2. commodity	( )	7. diploma	( )	12. solemnly	( )
3. confuse	( )	8. firm	( )	13. testimonial	( )
4. creature	( )	9. joint	( )	14. token	( )
5. curious	( )	10. parting	( )	15. wisdom	( )

a. 生き物　　　d. 感傷的な　　　g. 混同する　　　j. 感謝状、推薦状　m. 学位記、卒業証書
b. 裏庭、近所　e. 関節、継ぎ目　h. 知恵、分別　　k. しるし、あかし　n. 厳粛に
c. 会社、商会　f. 好奇心の強い　i. 欲望、要求　　l. （人との）別れ　o. 役に立つ物、商品

Listening Tips

人名や地名などの聞き取り

　映画『オズの魔法使』は、ドロシーが故郷カンザスに戻る冒険を描いたものでした。ドロシーは Dorothy と綴り /dɔ́ːrəθi/ と発音することは、みなさんにはすっかりおなじみのはずですが、改めて考えてみると、ドロシーの「シ」は th /θ/ ですから、日本語的な発音と英語本来の発音が、ずいぶんと違うことに気付かされます。また、カンザスは Kansas /kǽnzəs/ ですから、s が /z/ とも /s/ とも発音されます。このように、英語を「読む・聞く・話す・書く」すべての場合において、人名や地名はなかなかやっかいですから、普段から意識するようにしましょう。また、いわゆるカタカナ語が本来の英語の発音と全く異なる場合が多いことにも注意が必要です。

Exercises　　　　　　　　　　　　　　　　　📺 53 Ⓢ 68

次の人名・地名・カタカナ語を英語で表記し、発音しなさい。

1. ナオミ 人名 ( )	6. シドニー 地名 ( )
2. マイケル 人名 ( )	7. キャリア カナ ( )
3. テレサ 人名 ( )	8. ゼリー カナ ( )
4. ジュネーブ 地名 ( )	9. サクセス カナ ( )
5. バチカン 地名 ( )	10. アレルギー カナ ( )

Part 1 写真の場面を最も適切に表している音声を選びなさい。　🇹2 54　Ⓢ 69

1. Ⓐ Ⓑ Ⓒ Ⓓ

Part 2 問いかけに対する最も適切な応答を選びなさい。　🇹2 55-56　Ⓢ 70-71

 偉大なオズの魔法使いは実はただの人間で、からくりの演出によって魔法使いらしく見せていただけだった。それを知ったドロシーの台詞。

2. Ⓐ Ⓑ Ⓒ

 正体を現した「魔法使い」は気球でドロシーをカンザスに連れ帰ろうとするが、ドロシーが乗り損ねて帰れなくなってしまう。ライオンは…

3. Ⓐ Ⓑ Ⓒ

Part 3 会話を聞き、設問に答えなさい。　🇹2 57　Ⓢ 72
　　　　（登場話者：Dorothy, Scarecrow, Glinda）

 Part 2 の 2 に続く場面。もう家に帰れなくなったと泣いているドロシーのもとに、良い魔女グリンダが現れて助言をする。

4. What does Scarecrow think that Glinda will do for Dorothy?
　(A) She will help Dorothy.
　(B) She will go to Kansas to ask for some help.
　(C) She will give Dorothy a big hand.
　(D) She will find someone who can help Dorothy.

5. What does Glinda say to Dorothy?
   (A) Dorothy has to help Scarecrow.
   (B) Dorothy should not stay any longer.
   (C) Dorothy does not need anybody's help.
   (D) Dorothy cannot get back to Kansas.

6. Why didn't Glinda tell Dorothy earlier that she had the power to go back to Kansas?
   (A) Dorothy had to become aware of it by herself.
   (B) Dorothy was already aware of it.
   (C) Dorothy was too ready to believe.
   (D) Dorothy did not want to go back to Kansas.

Part 4 ドロシーの話を聞き、設問に答えなさい。　 58　 73

 Part 3 に続く場面。ドロシーは一連の冒険を通して重要なことを学んだと言うのだが、それはどんなことだったのだろうか。

7. According to Dorothy, what was not enough to get back home?
   (A) Wanting to be with her relatives
   (B) Being kinder to her uncle and aunt
   (C) Helping with her uncle's firm
   (D) Cutting the grass in the backyard

8. Where can Dorothy's dearest wish be found?
   (A) In a faraway land over the rainbow
   (B) In her late father's garden
   (C) At the lost and found
   (D) At home

9. What does it mean when Dorothy says "I never really lost it to begin with"?
   (A) She was looking for something she already had.
   (B) She should look in other places.
   (C) She never got lost.
   (D) She did not have it from the beginning.

Dictation

音声を聞き、適切な語句を空所に書き入れなさい。

Part 1

T2 54　S 69

1. (A) The girl is (^{1}) the (^{2}) with a broom.

  (B) The girl is (^{3}) (^{4}) a broomstick.

  (C) The girl is (^{5}) a broom.

  (D) The flowers are in (^{6}) (^{7}).

Part 2

T2 55-56　S 70-71

2. You are a very (^{1}) (^{2})!

  (A) Oh, no, my dear. I'm a very (^{3}) (^{4}).

  (B) Pay (^{5}) (^{6}) to that man behind the (^{7}).

  (C) You just had a (^{8}) (^{9}).

3. Stay with us, then, Dorothy. We all love you. We don't want you to go.

  (A) Why have you come back?

  (B) Oh, that's very (^{10}) (^{11}) you.

  (C) (^{12}) (^{13}) and come back tomorrow!

Part 3

Dorothy: Oh, Scarecrow, what am I (^{1}) (^{2}) do?

Scarecrow: Look! Here's someone who can help you.

Dorothy: Oh, (^{3}) you help me? (^{4}) you help me?

Glinda: You don't (^{5}) (^{6}) be helped (^{7}) (^{8}).

You've always had the (^{9}) to go back to Kansas.

Dorothy: I have?

Scarecrow: Then why didn't you tell her before?

Glinda: Because she (^{10}) (^{11}) (^{12}) me.

She had to (^{13}) (^{14}) for herself.

Part 4

Well, I think that it wasn't (^{1}) just to (^{2}) (^{3}) see

Uncle Henry and Auntie Em. And it's that, if I ever (^{4}) (^{5})

(^{6}) my heart's (^{7}) again, I won't look any (^{8}) than

my own (^{9}). Because if it isn't there, I never really lost it (^{10})

(^{11}) (^{12}). Is that right?

10. How can I _____ thank you enough?
　　(A) ever
　　(B) almost
　　(C) very
　　(D) much

11. You are confusing courage _____
　　wisdom.
　　(A) to
　　(B) with
　　(C) from
　　(D) about

12. And remember, my sentimental friend, that
　　a heart is not judged by how much you
　　love, _____ by how much you are loved
　　by others.
　　(A) as
　　(B) because
　　(C) and
　　(D) but

13. The only way to get Dorothy back to
　　Kansas is _____ me to take her there
　　myself.
　　(A) for
　　(B) to
　　(C) by
　　(D) with

14. Oh, dear. That is _____ wonderful to
　　be true.
　　(A) so
　　(B) such
　　(C) too
　　(D) enough

 からくりがばれてしまった「魔法使い」は、約束をどうしてくれるのかと皆に問い詰められるが、得意の詭弁で窮地を逃れることに成功する。

Why, ---15--- can have a brain. That's a very mediocre commodity.

Every pusillanimous creature that crawls on the earth, or slinks through

slimy seas ---16--- a brain!

Back where I come from we have universities, seats of great

learning, ---17--- men go to become great thinkers. And when they come

out, they think deep thoughts, and with no more brains than you have.

But, they have one thing you haven't got! A ---18---!

Notes:

mediocre「平凡な、二流の」**pusillanimous**「臆病な、気弱な」

15. (A) anybody
    (B) somebody
    (C) nobody
    (D) not everybody

16. (A) had
    (B) has
    (C) have
    (D) having

17. (A) when
    (B) what
    (C) which
    (D) where

18. (A) diploma
    (B) medal
    (C) testimonial
    (D) token

ドロシーがカンザスのエムおばさんのもとに帰る場面は、原作ではどのように描かれているだろうか。映画と比べてみよう。

"The Silver Shoes," said the Good Witch, "have wonderful powers. And one of the most curious things about them is that they can carry you to any place in the world in three steps, and each step will be made in the wink of an eye. All you have to do is to knock the heels together three times and command the shoes to carry you wherever you wish to go."

"If that is so," said the child, joyfully, "I will ask them to carry me back to Kansas at once."

She threw her arms around the Lion's neck and kissed him, patting his big head tenderly. Then she kissed the Tin Woodman, who was weeping in a way most dangerous to his joints. But she hugged the soft, stuffed body of the Scarecrow in her arms instead of kissing his painted face, and found she was crying herself at this sorrowful parting from her loving comrades.

—[1]—.

Glinda the Good stepped down from her ruby throne to give the little girl a good-bye kiss, and Dorothy thanked her for all the kindness she had shown to her friends and herself.

—[2]—.

Dorothy now took Toto up solemnly in her arms, and having said one last good-bye she clapped the heels of her shoes together three times, saying, "Take me home to Aunt Em!"

Instantly she was whirling through the air, so swiftly that all she could see or feel was the wind whistling past her ears.

—[3]—.

At length, however, she sat up and looked about her.

"Good gracious!" she cried.

For she was sitting on the broad Kansas prairie, and just before her was the new farm-house Uncle Henry built after the cyclone had carried away the old one. Uncle Henry was milking the cows in the barnyard, and Toto had jumped out of her arms and was running toward the barn, barking joyously.

Dorothy stood up and found she was in her stocking-feet. For the Silver Shoes had fallen off in her flight through the air, and were lost forever in the desert.

Aunt Em had just come out of the house to water the cabbages when she looked up and saw Dorothy running toward her.

—[4]—.

"My darling child!" she cried, folding the little girl in her arms and covering her face with kisses; "where in the world did you come from?"

"From the Land of Oz," said Dorothy, gravely. "And here is Toto, too. And oh, Aunt Em! I'm so glad to be at home again!"

Notes:
at length 「ついに、ようやく」 **milk** 「乳絞りをする」 **gravely** 「厳粛に、真剣に」

19. What must Dorothy do to get back to Kansas?
    (A) Knock at the door of the Good Witch's house
    (B) Command the Good Witch to carry her there
    (C) Wink at her friends and say good-bye to them
    (D) Tap the heels of her shoes a certain number of times

20. In the text, the word "comrades" in paragraph 3, line 5, is closest in meaning to
    (A) companions
    (B) patrons
    (C) relatives
    (D) siblings

21. What was Uncle Henry doing when Dorothy came back?
    (A) He was milking the goats.
    (B) He was working in the barnyard.
    (C) He was watering the cabbages.
    (D) He was building a new farm-house.

22. What is NOT true about the passage?
    (A) Dorothy did not kiss Scarecrow when she left the Land of Oz.
    (B) Toto was carried whirling together with Dorothy in the air.
    (C) Dorothy was barefoot when she got back to Kansas.
    (D) Toto seemed happy to be finally at home again.

23. In which of the positions marked [1], [2], [3] and [4] does the following sentence best belong?
    "The Silver Shoes took but three steps, and then she stopped so suddenly that she rolled over upon the grass several times before she knew where she was."
    (A) [1]
    (B) [2]
    (C) [3]
    (D) [4]

仮定法

---

1. If you **were** King, you **wouldn't** be afraid of anything.
2. Even if I **had told** her before, she **would not have believed** me.
3. Dorothy felt **as if** she **were** going up in a balloon.

　仮定法は、事実をありのままに述べるのではなく、現実とは違うことを想像して述べるときや、話し手の願望を表すときに使われる表現方法です。本来使うべき時制よりも1つ前の時制を用いているということがポイントです。具体的には、現在のことを表すのに過去形を用い、過去のことを表すのに過去完了形を用います。ここでは、仮定法でよく使われる、以下の3つの形式を確認しましょう。

仮定法過去：現在の事実に反することを述べる
「もし（今）〜なら、〜だろう」
If ＋主語＋動詞の過去形 , 主語＋ would / could / might ＋動詞の原形 .
　If I knew her e-mail address, I would contact her.

仮定法過去完了：過去の事実に反することを述べる
「もし（過去に）〜なら、〜だっただろう」
If ＋主語＋ had ＋動詞の過去分詞形 , 主語＋ would / could / might ＋ have ＋動詞の過去分詞形 .
　If I had had more time then, I would have talked with you about this problem.

仮定法現在：話し手の願望や要求を表す
「〜することを 要求する / 提案する / 忠告する など」
主語＋ demand / propose / advise など＋ that ＋主語＋ (should) ＋動詞の原形 .
　I demanded that he tell me the truth.

Exercises

(　　) 内から適切な語句を選びましょう。

1. If I (had / had had) wings, I would fly away from here.

2. If my boss (did not help / had not helped) me, I might have failed.

3. Although she knows nothing about art, she speaks (as / even) if she did.

4. I wish I (can turn / could turn) back the clock and do it all over again.

5. It is high time you (go / went) to bed.

6. She suggested that he (go / went) see a doctor immediately.

名作映画で TOEIC® (4)　めざせ！470 —『オズの魔法使』
[Boost your skills for the TOEIC® Test with *The Wizard of Oz*]

2020 年 1 月 15 日　初　版

著　者 ©　中　郷　　慶
　　　　　　小　沢　　茂
　　　　　　太　田　晶　子
　　　　　　Isabelle Bilodeau
　　　　　　Beverley Curran

発 行 者　佐　々　木　　元

発 行 所　株式会社　英　　宝　　社
　〒101-0032 東京都千代田区岩本町 2-7-7
　☎ [03] (5833) 5870-1　FAX [03] (5833) 5872

ISBN978-4-269-66047-2 C3582
［組版：小沢　茂／製版・印刷・製本：萩原印刷株式会社／表紙デザイン：興亜産業㈱］

 CD 付